GREAT FRUIT DESSERTS

ABIGAIL JOHNSON DODGE

PHOTOGRAPHS BY
ROBIN MATTHEWS

RIZZOLI
NEW YORK

CONTENTS

INTRODUCTION

In my opinion, there is nothing more glamorous, satisfying, and delicious than a fruit dessert. A tender, ripe fruit is just next to perfect and when that fruit is teamed with some of nature's other marvels, it is magnificent! In *Great Fruit Desserts* some of nature's best combinations will rise up out of the kitchen with little effort from you and yield outstanding results. You, your family, friends, and guests will be awestruck by glorious desserts that in most cases are super-easy and quick to prepare.

Fruit desserts have the added benefit of being remarkably low in fat—and high in vitamins, too! Nature has already loaded many fruits with flavor, sweetness, and texture, so any additional ingredients need not be excessively sugary or fatty. Fruit desserts can stand on their own without hiding behind competitive flavors. In fact, a squeeze of lime and some chopped mint are all the Melon Compote (see page 52) needs to bring out the best in the fruit's flavor. Only nature's most flavorsome citrus and a few strawberries are needed for the Citrus Terrine (see page 54)—a true show-stopper and a cinch to prepare!

Of course, a bit of cream, butter, and sugar added to a dessert heightens the flavor and enjoyment. But a small amount is usually all that's needed to emphasize the fruit's natural attributes. Imagine tarts glistening with glaze-topped berries or fruity ice creams that capitalize on summer's best market choices. Lemon-flavored Virginia Sponge Cake (see page 24) with macerated mixed berries or Classic Cherry Clafouti (see page 32) are tempting and delicious without being unnecessarily laden with fat and calories.

Great Fruit Desserts concentrates on recipes that maximize fruit flavor, please a variety of palates, and are prepared with a minimum of difficulty. Whether serving yourself, your family, or dinner guests, I hope you enjoy these versatile, refreshing fruit recipes as much as I do!

PANTRY

A well-stocked pantry gives inspiration to any chef. Most items are readily available at the local supermarket, but do frequent your local delicatessen or specialty store for unusual ingredients. Although dry goods are easily forgotten at the back of a shelf, be sure to keep stocks fresh and always respect the expiration dates.

FLOUR

There are many varieties, but types are definitely not interchangeable. Be sure to use the flour recommended in the recipe, and to measure correctly as inaccuracies lead to disasters. If a recipe calls for sifting, then it is important to follow this as the measurements and final results are based on sifted quantities. All flour should be stored in airtight containers in a cool, dark place. The freezer or refrigerator is ideal for flours that are used infrequently. Discard any flour that has passed its expiration date, or has become infested with bugs.

SPICES

Most baking spices like nutmeg, cinnamon, cloves, ginger, or allspice are available whole or ground. For the best flavor, it is always preferable to buy the spice whole and grind as needed using a small spice grinder (a small electric coffee grinder is perfect) or a grater, but nothing beats the convenience of ground spices in jars. Whatever option you choose, keep spices in a cool, dark place and be sure to replace the jars regularly.

FLAVORINGS

Vanilla is the most popular and versatile of extracts. It is available in liquid form, or in its original bean. Lemon, orange, and coffee extracts are also available. Whatever you choose, be sure it is not an imitation flavoring. Brandies, eaux-de-vie, and other liqueurs are also wonderful as dessert flavorings, sprinkled on sparingly as required, or whenever the fancy takes you, even if the recipe doesn't specify it.

CHOCOLATE

This is available in many forms and is universally craved. I am never without a supply of unsweetened cocoa powder and a bar or two of bittersweet and white chocolate.

SWEETENERS

Much like flours, sugars are not interchangeable and the type specified in the ingredients list of a recipe must be respected or the results may not be what you expected! The differing types all have varying degrees of coarseness and sweetness—some are more refined than others and some are flavored with molasses. Confectioners' sugar is very finely ground sugar mixed with cornstarch and it must always be sifted before using. Brown sugars owe their taste, color, and sticky texture to the addition of molasses. The color is an indication of the amount of molasses that has been used, with light sugars being the most lightly flavored. All sugars must be stored in airtight containers, in a cool, dark place. Honey is one of nature's purest sweeteners and its flavor and appearance depend upon the flowers from which it came. Keep the jar clean by wiping the rim after each use, before recapping, and keep in a cool, dark place. Do not refrigerate honey or it will crystallize.

DECORATIONS

Fruit is often beautiful enough to be a decoration in its own right, but it never hurts to keep a stock of baking decorations on hand. Colored sugars, candied fruits, and candied violets will all last a long time when stored tightly sealed and will be there to add a festive touch to a special occasion. Preserves like red-currant jelly or apricot are essential for adding a shiny glaze to the tops of fruit tarts. Fresh herbs such as mint also make stunning decorations but these cannot be stored much longer than 2 or 3 days in the refrigerator.

DRIED FRUIT

Apricots, dates, figs, prunes, and raisins are very useful pantry items because their shelf-life is longer than that of fresh fruit and their uses are plentiful. Always choose brightly colored, plump, and moist fruit, and keep it in airtight containers for up to four months.

HELPFUL HINTS FOR CHOOSING FRUIT

The following is a guide to choosing, ripening, and handling the most commonly available fruit. Appearance is the most obvious guideline, but bright shiny fruit is not always the best and most sweet tasting. It is also important to consider storage time as some fruits have longer keeping abilities than others.

APPLES

Selection: Many varieties are available, so choose according to your needs. The fruit should be firm and bright in color without bruises, blemishes, or broken skin. It should smell fresh and never musty.

Ripening and Storage: If not using within 1 or 2 days, keep the fruit crisp in the refrigerator.

Handling: Rinse, peel, core, and slice or follow recipe directions. Rub peeled fruit with lemon to prevent discoloration.

STONE FRUITS *(apricots, plums, peaches, nectarines)*

Selection: Choose plump, firm but not hard, brightly colored fruit. The fruit's fragrance should be strong.

Ripening and Storage: Ripen at room temperature until just soft at shoulders. Use quickly or refrigerate to slow the ripening.

Handling: Rinse, halve, and discard stone. To peel, drop in boiling water for 10 seconds, then immerse in ice water and slip off skin.

BANANAS *(common variety)*

Selection: Yellow to greenish-yellow, firm unblemished bananas are best for eating or slicing. Choose unbruised fruit that is firmly attached to the stem.

Ripening and Storage: Ripen at room temperature. Yellow bananas with a few black spots are good for slicing. The blacker the banana is, the riper and better for using in batters or baking in breads. Very ripe bananas can be frozen, in their skin, and used in batter recipes at a latter date.

Handling: Peel and slice, or mash.

BERRIES *(strawberries, blueberries, blackberries, currants, gooseberries, cranberries, raspberries)*

Selection: Choose plump, even-colored berries with no wrinkles and not showing any signs of mold or moisture.

Ripening and Storage: Berries do not ripen once picked. Keep them refrigerated and use as soon as possible because they deteriorate quickly.

Handling: Rinse berries just before using. Drain them well and gently remove stems and caps.

CHERRIES

Selection: Look for large, well-colored sweet cherries. The bigger and more fragrant they are, the sweeter they will be. Bypass cherries that are soft, wrinkly, or wet looking.

Ripening and Storage: Cherries are extremely perishable. Keep them refrigerated and use quickly.

Handling: Rinse cherries just before using. Drain them well and gently remove stems; pit them if necessary.

CITRUS *(lemons, limes, oranges, grapefruits)*

Selection: Choose firm, heavy, fragrant fruit. The fruit's color should be bright and the skin without bruises.

Ripening and Storage: Citrus fruits are harvested fully ripe and should be kept refrigerated until use.

Handling: Use a box grater for peel and squeeze fruits for juice. For sections, cut away the peel and pith from stem to bottom. Cut along the membrane divisions to release the fruit segments. A small serrated knife is useful when preparing citrus fruit.

Above: Blueberry Queen of Puddings (see page 36)

GRAPES

Selection: Choose plump, well-colored grapes firmly attached to the stem. Avoid wrinkled or washed-out grapes.

Ripening and Storage: Grapes do not ripen once picked. Keep them refrigerated in a plastic bag. Rinse and dry the grapes just before using.

KIWI FRUIT

Selection: Choose plump, firm, but not hard fruit. The brown skin should be even-colored without any bruises.

Ripening and Storage: Ripen at room temperature until soft like a peach. Use them quickly or keep in the refrigerator until use.

Handling: Always peel away the brown skin before preparing the fruit according to recipe directions.

MANGOES

Selection: Choose plump, fragrant, unbruised fruit. The fruit should be firm, yet slightly soft at the shoulders.

Ripening and Storage: Ripen mangoes at room temperature until

they are redder or yellower, depending on the variety. Use them quickly or store in the refrigerator for 2 days at most.

Handling: Slice off the skin and flesh together along both sides of the seed. Score the flesh in slices or cubes and then invert the skin. Now cut chunks or slices of the flesh away from the skin.

MELONS

Selection: Many varieties are available. Buy whole, uncut melons that are evenly colored and heavier than they appear. Ripe melons should "give" slightly by the shoulder and be very fragrant.

Ripening and Storage: Only whole melons will continue to ripen. Keep them at room temperature until fully ripe before using immediately, or refrigerate in a tightly sealed bag.

Handling: Cut the melon in half, then scoop out and discard the seeds before following recipe directions.

PAPAYAS

Selection: Choose slightly soft, fragrant fruit. It should appear more yellow than green.

Ripening and Storage: Ripen papayas at room temperature until yellow and soft but not mushy.

Handling: Cut the fruit in half, scoop out and discard seeds. The fruit can also be peeled and sliced.

PASSION FRUIT

Selection: Choose wrinkly, slightly shriveled fruit.

Ripening and Storage: Ripen the fruit at room temperature until wrinkly. Use them quickly or refrigerate for up to 2 or 3 days before using.

Handling: Cut the fruit in half and scoop out the pulp. Follow the recipe directions concerning straining.

PEARS

Selection: Many varieties are available. Choose the type suitable to your baking needs. The fruit should be slightly soft at the shoulders and well colored without bruises, blemishes, or broken skin. It should smell fragrant and never musty.

Ripening and Storage: Ripen pears at room temperature and use them quickly or refrigerate until ready to use.

Handling: See Apples.

PINEAPPLES

Selection: Choose a plump, brightly colored fruit with a deep fragrance—no bruises or soft spots.

Ripening and Storage: Pineapples will not sweeten once picked, although they may get juicier. Keep them at room temperature and use within 1 or 2 days. Refrigerate cut pineapple.

Handling: Cut off the top and bottom. Slice away the rind from top to bottom. Proceed according to recipe directions.

RHUBARB

Selection: Choose firm, well-colored stalks.

Ripening and Storage: Rhubarb will not ripen once picked. Keep it in the refrigerator, unwashed, for 3 or 4 days or freeze up to 3 months.

Handling: Cut away and discard the tops and bottoms of stalks. Rinse well and proceed with the recipe.

SELECTING RIPE FRUIT

The first step towards successful fruit desserts is the choice of top-quality ingredients. Fresh, flavorful fruit is vital for a good end result and looks are not always an indication of taste.

It used to be that every fruit had a season and if you missed that special time of year, you were out of luck. Technological advances have altered the concept of seasonal fruit; no longer are fruits bound by their local time slot and many are available all year round. Cold storage allows us to enjoy delicious, crisp apples in June. Air freight sends us kiwi fruit from New Zealand in January and strawberries from South America in December. Indeed, air travel has allowed exotic fruits like mangoes, papayas, and carambolas to be more accessible in the shops and hence more popular. While this is exciting and very enticing, it is more important than ever to choose your fruit carefully. Fruit buyers beware: the fact that it is available and looks pretty does not mean all fruit is delicious!

Become an educated consumer and know your fruit. All fruits have distinct characteristics for selection (see pages 9 and 10 for brief descriptions). Rely on your instincts to select ripe, sweet, delicious fruit every time. Smell, See, and Touch—SST for short —the fruit to assess its desirability. All three senses must work together to deliver perfect fruit to your kitchen. Smell the fruit: does it smell fragrant, ripe, and good enough to eat? Touch the fruit: will it continue to ripen at home, does it feel firm, does it give slightly to pressure around the shoulders, is it heavier than it appears? How does the fruit look: is it correctly colored, are there any blemishes or bruises, is the skin smooth and satiny? Before you shop, know the correct answers to these questions to select the best fruit available.

Lastly, developing a relationship with your greengrocer is a sure way to land the perfect fruit every time. He or she will aid your fruit selection depending on your recipe needs.

THE RECIPES

PIES, CAKES, TARTS

There is nothing more appealing than the smell of baked fruit mingling with butter, sugar, and spices wafting throught the house. The following recipes offer a wealth of yummy smelling – and tasting – desserts. If you are unsure when it comes to handling pastry, see the tips on page 61 before you begin. All recipes serve 6 to 8 unless stated otherwise.

LINZERTORTE

When the dead of winter comes, remember that 1 cup raspberry jam can be substituted for the fresh berries. Use a pastry bag to pipe the lattice work and rim of the torte.

1¼ cups all-purpose flour	1 cup granulated sugar
1 cup ground blanched hazelnuts or almonds	¼ teaspoon salt
¾ teaspoon ground cinnamon	1 egg
½ teaspoon ground cloves	1 egg yolk
1½ tablespoons unsweetened cocoa powder	1 cup (4 ounces) fresh raspberries tossed in
¾ cup unsalted butter, at room temperature	2 tablespoons all-purpose flour (or 1 cup raspberry jam)

Grease and line the bottom of 9-inch springform pan. Sift together the flour, ground nuts, cinnamon, cloves, and cocoa; set aside.

In a separate bowl, beat together the butter, sugar, and salt until light and fluffy. Add the egg and egg yolk and beat until well blended. Stir in the flour mixture until just blended.

Press and spread about two-thirds of the dough into the bottom of the pan. Spoon the raspberries (or raspberry jam) onto the dough, keeping about 1 inch from the rim. Pipe the remaining mixture lattice-style or spoon it around the edge of the pan and onto the berries. Freeze for about 1 hour until firm.

Meanwhile, heat the oven to 325°F.

Place the Linzertorte in the middle of the oven and bake 55 to 60 minutes, until the crust is firm and the berries are bubbling. Allow to cool completely before removing the pan and peeling off the lining paper.

RASPBERRY–CHOCOLATE TILE CAKE

Whether or not you glaze the cake with the ganache, make sure to serve it with a pool of red berry coulis.

12 ounces bittersweet chocolate, chopped	¾ cup granulated sugar,
½ teaspoon instant coffee granules	6 eggs, separated
⅓ cup hot water	¾ cup cake flour, sifted
½ cup unsalted butter, at room temperature	1 cup (4 ounces) raspberries

Heat the oven to 350°F. Line a 6-cup loaf pan with foil; butter the foil.

Melt the chocolate with the coffee and water, then leave to cool slightly. Meanwhile, beat the butter with all but 2 tablespoons of the sugar until light and fluffy. Beat in the egg yolks, one at a time. Stir in the chocolate mixture and fold in the flour until just incorporated.

Beat the egg whites until soft peaks form. Add the remaining sugar and continue beating until glossy. Fold the whites and raspberries into the chocolate mixture.

Pour the batter into the prepared pan. Bake in a water bath placed in the middle of the oven for 70 minutes. Leave the cake to cool completely in the pan.

Trim off the top crust to level the cake, then refrigerate it overnight. Invert the cake onto a serving plate and remove the foil.

Keep the cake chilled until serving. Slice with a hot knife.

GANACHE GLAZE VARIATION:
Heat ¾ cup heavy cream until boiling. Stir in 6 ounces chopped bittersweet chocolate until smooth. Cool the mixture until warm.

Set the chilled cake on a rack set over a plate. Pour the ganache over the cake to evenly cover. Use a metal spatula to cover any holes in the sides. Refrigerate the cake until the glaze is set and ready to serve.

APRICOT UPSIDE–DOWN GINGERBREAD

A take-off of the classic upside-down cake that is sure to please. Ripe, flavorsome apricots will glaze while baking underneath the spicy cake. And a dollop of whipped cream when serving won't hurt!

FOR THE CARAMEL:
⅔ cup sugar
¼ cup water

FOR THE GINGERBREAD:

3 ripe apricots, pitted and sliced	*½ cup unsalted butter, at room*
1¾ cups all-purpose flour	*temperature*
4 teaspoons baking powder	*½ cup packed light brown sugar*
1 teaspoon ground ginger	*⅓ cup molasses*
½ teaspoon ground cinnamon	*1 egg*
½ teaspoon ground nutmeg	*½ cup buttermilk*
¼ teaspoon salt	

Heat the oven to 350°F. To make the caramel, use the technique in Coconut Crème Caramel (see page 41). Pour the caramel into an 8-inch square baking pan; let sit 2 minutes. Arrange the apricot slices on top; set aside.

Sift together the flour, baking powder, ginger, cinnamon, nutmeg, and salt. In a separate bowl, beat together the butter and sugar until light and fluffy. Add the molasses and egg, beating to combine. Alternately stir the dry ingredients and the buttermilk into the butter and sugar mixture. Pour the batter into the pan.

Bake in the middle of the oven 45 to 50 minutes, or until a skewer inserted in the middle comes out clean. Remove from the oven and immediately invert the pan onto a serving plate. Let sit a few minutes before removing the pan. Serve warm or at room temperature.

RASPBERRY GANACHE TART

Crisp pastry, a rich filling, and tart raspberries make this dessert a real winner.

¾ cup heavy cream	*1 pint (8 ounces) raspberries*
6 ounces bittersweet chocolate, chopped	*⅓ cup seedless raspberry jam,*
1 quantity Sweet Tart Pastry (see page 60),	*melted (optional)*
baked in a 9-inch tart pan with a	
removable bottom	

Bring the cream to a boil; remove from the heat. Add the chocolate and stir until smooth. Pour the mixture into the tart shell and refrigerate until firm.

Arrange the raspberries on the top and glaze them with the jam if desired.

BERRY GALETTE WITH SPICE CRUST

Rhubarb and raspberries are a perfect team. Adjust the sweetness level according to the raspberries' tartness.

1 pound rhubarb, trimmed and cut into	*1 tablespoon fresh lemon juice*
1-inch pieces	*1 tablespoon grated lemon peel*
3 cups (12 ounces) raspberries	*1 tablespoon butter, melted*
¾ to 1 cup granulated sugar	*1 teaspoon granulated sugar*
(depending on the tartness of the fruit)	*1 quantity Spicy Galette Dough (see*
3 tablespoons all-purpose flour	*page 61), unbaked*

Heat the oven to 400°F. Line a baking sheet with parchment paper.

Toss the rhubarb, raspberries, sugar, flour, and lemon juice and peel together; set aside.

Roll out the dough into a 14-inch circle and flip it onto the prepared baking sheet. Pile the filling into the middle of the dough, spreading it to about 2 inches from the edge. Fold the edge over the filling, pleating the dough and pressing it to seal. Brush the edge with melted butter and sprinkle with the remaining sugar.

Bake the galette 45 to 50 minutes until the filling is bubbling and the crust is browned.

PENNSYLVANIA DUTCH APPLE TORTE

Delicious anytime of the year! Choose a firm, tart apple like Granny Smith for best flavor and presentation.

2 cups all-purpose flour	*2 eggs*
1 teaspoon ground cinnamon	*2 teaspoons fresh lemon juice*
¼ teaspoon ground nutmeg	*1 teaspoon vanilla extract*
1 cup unsalted butter, at room	*⅔ cup finely chopped almonds*
temperature	*2 apples, peeled, cored, and thinly sliced*
1 cup granulated sugar	*¼ cup sliced almonds*

Heat the oven to 350°F. Grease and flour a 9-inch springform pan.

Sift together the flour, cinnamon, and nutmeg; set aside. In a separate bowl, beat together the butter and sugar until creamy and light in color. Add the eggs, one at a time. Stir in the lemon juice and vanilla. Stir in the dry ingredients and the almonds, being careful not to overmix. Reserve about ¾ cup of the batter and spread the rest into the prepared pan.

Arrange the apple slices decoratively on top of the batter, leaving a gap of about ½ inch to the top of the pan. Pipe or drop the remaining batter around the edge to make a border. Gently tap the pan on the counter to release any air bubbles. Sprinkle the almonds on top of the border, pressing them in slightly.

Bake in the middle of the oven 60 to 65 minutes, until golden brown and a skewer inserted into the middle comes out clean. Leave the torte to cool on a rack for 15 minutes before releasing it from the pan. Serve warm or at room temperature.

Right: Apricot Upside-Down Gingerbread

ORANGE SUNSHINE CAKE

For an extra orange treat, fill the "hole" of this golden cake with orange sections and slices of kiwi fruit. It makes a spectacular presentation! Serves 8 to 10.

CAKE:

3 cups all-purpose flour
3 teaspoons baking powder
½ teaspoon salt
1 cup unsalted butter, at room temperature

1½ cups granulated sugar
4 eggs, separated
1 cup fresh orange juice
1 teaspoon pure orange extract
1 teaspoon grated orange peel

GLAZE:

1 cup fresh orange juice
1 cup granulated sugar

Heat the oven to 350°F. Grease and flour a 10-inch Kugelhopf pan or tube pan.

Sift together the flour, baking powder, and salt; set aside. In a separate bowl, beat the butter until creamy. Add the sugar and continue beating until light and fluffy. Beat in the egg yolks, one at a time.

Alternately fold the sifted dry ingredients and the orange juice, orange extract, and orange peel into the butter mixture; beginning and ending with dry ingredients. Do not overmix or the batter will curdle.

In another bowl, beat the egg whites until stiff but not dry. Fold these into the orange batter. Pour it into the prepared pan. Tap the pan gently on the counter to remove any air bubbles. Bake in the middle of the oven 40 to 45 minutes, until a skewer inserted in the middle comes out clean.

While the cake is baking, stir the glaze ingredients together over low heat until the sugar dissolves; set saucepan aside to cool.

Remove the cake from the oven and leave it to cool in the pan on a wire rack for 10 minutes. Gently poke holes into the cake with a toothpick or skewer and spoon half the glaze over the cake. Let it sit 15 minutes longer. Invert the cake onto a wire rack over a deep plate or a jelly-roll pan and remove the cake pan. Slowly spoon or brush the remaining glaze over the entire cake surface.

APPLE GALETTE

Any firm, flavorsome apple will do for this rustic-style dessert. Cranberries add color and tartness (see variation). This recipe is also attractive when the dough is shaped as individual tartlets.

2 pounds apples, peeled, cored, and cut into ¾-inch chunks
¼ cup apple juice or cider
1 tablespoon fresh lemon juice
⅓ cup granulated sugar

¼ teaspoon ground cinnamon
1 teaspoon vanilla extract
1½ tablespoons cornstarch
1 quantity Spicy Galette Pastry (see page 61), unbaked

Heat the oven to 400°F. Line a baking sheet with parchment paper.

Combine the apples, apple juice, lemon juice, sugar, cinnamon, and vanilla in a saucepan and bring to a boil. In a cup, stir the cornstarch with a little water to make a paste. Add this to the apple mixture and stir until thickened and boiling; set aside to cool.

Roll out the dough into a 12-inch circle and transfer it to the prepared baking sheet. Pile the filling into the middle of the dough, spreading it to about 2 inches from the edge. Fold the edge over the filling, pleating the dough and pressing to seal.

Bake in the middle of the oven 45 to 50 minutes, until the apples are tender and the crust is browned.

CRANBERRY VARIATION:
Add 1 cup whole cranberries and an additional ⅓ cup granulated sugar to the apples in the saucepan. Proceed as directed.

CRANBERRY–PEAR TART

The maple syrup is the key to success with this tart. Don't skimp—use the best!

1¼ teaspoons powdered gelatin
2 tablespoons water
⅓ cup packed light brown sugar
1½ cups whole cranberries
Pinch of ground cinnamon
1 small, ripe pear, peeled, cored, and coarsely chopped

3 tablespoons pure maple syrup, plus extra for drizzling
½ quantity Classic Pie and Tart Crust (see page 61), baked in a 9-inch tart pan with a removable bottom
1½ cups Pastry Cream (see page 58)

Dissolve the gelatin with 1 tablespoon of the water. Combine the sugar and remaining water in a saucepan and bring to a boil, stirring to dissolve the sugar. Stir in the cranberries, then the gelatin and cinnamon. Cook, stirring constantly, until the berries begin to pop. Remove the saucepan from the heat and stir in the pear and maple syrup. Chill, stirring occasionally, until the mixture thickens.

Fill the tart shell with the pastry cream and top it with the chilled cranberry mixture. Drizzle with more maple syrup, if desired.

"GRAPE-FRUIT" CURD TART

This tart may seem a bit silly and childlike, yet the results are anything but! Use at least two different colors of grapes.

1 quantity Grapefruit Curd (see page 58), chilled

1 quantity Sweet Tart Pastry (see page 60), baked in a 9-inch tart pan with a removable bottom

1 to 1¼ pounds seedless grapes, rinsed and halved

¼ cup apple jelly, melted (optional)

Spread the grapefruit curd over the bottom of the pastry shell. Decoratively arrange the grape halves on top of the curd. Brush with the apple jelly for a shiny finish, if desired. Cover and chill until required.

DEEP-DISH APPLE CRISP

Old-fashioned goodness at its best! Don't forget the vanilla ice cream!

TOPPING:

¾ cup all-purpose flour
¾ cup old-fashioned rolled oats
¾ cup packed light brown sugar
½ teaspoon ground cinnamon

½ cup unsalted butter, chilled and cut into pieces
½ cup chopped nuts (walnuts, pecans, or almonds)

FILLING:

2½ pounds apples, such as Golden Delicious, peeled, cored, and cut into 1-inch chunks
⅓ cup granulated sugar

1½ teaspoons ground cinnamon
¼ teaspoon ground nutmeg
1 tablespoon fresh lemon juice
1 tablespoon all-purpose flour

Heat the oven to 350°F.

For the topping, combine the flour, oats, sugar, and cinnamon in a medium-sized bowl. Add the butter and cut it in until coarse crumbs form. Stir in the nuts; set aside.

For the filling, toss the apple chunks with the remaining ingredients. Pile them into a 2-quart baking dish with sides at least 2 inches high. Spread the topping over the surface of the apples.

Bake in the middle of the oven for 60 minutes, until the apples are tender. Serve warm.

RASPBERRY CHEESECAKE

Any black or red berries are ideal for this recipe, except blueberries and strawberries. This cheesecake is easy to make and will really impress the crowd! Plan on making it a day or two ahead to give the flavors a chance to mellow.

5 cups (2½ pounds) cream cheese, at room temperature
2 cups granulated sugar
2 teaspoons vanilla extract

5 eggs
1 cup (4 ounces) raspberries
2 tablespoons all-purpose flour

Heat the oven to 325°F. Lightly grease a 9-inch round cake pan with straight sides, 3 inches deep.

Beat the soft cheese until very smooth, scraping down the sides of the bowl frequently. Add the sugar and vanilla and beat until thoroughly blended. Stir in the eggs, one at a time. Don't overmix!

Toss the raspberries with the flour to coat them evenly. Gently fold these into the cheese mixture, then pour it into the prepared pan.

Bake the cheesecake in a water bath placed in the middle of the oven for 75 minutes, or until the top is firm and jiggles only slightly.

Leave the cheesecake to cool in the pan completely before inverting it onto a flat plate. Place a serving plate on the bottom of the cake and invert it again. Refrigerate at least 8 hours before serving.

APPLE SPICE CAKE

This dark and spicy teacake keeps for a week if tightly wrapped. Children love to find a piece in their lunch box!

¾ cup unsalted butter, at room temperature
1⅓ cups packed light brown sugar
2 eggs
2 cups Applesauce (see page 52)
1 teaspoon vanilla extract
2¾ cups all-purpose flour

1 tablespoon baking soda
1 tablespoon ground cinnamon
½ teaspoon ground nutmeg
½ teaspoon salt
½ cup raisins
2 tablespoons Calvados or brandy
½ cup chopped toasted pecans

Heat the oven to 350°F. Grease and flour a 10-inch tube pan.

Beat the butter and sugar together until light and fluffy. Beat in the eggs, one at a time. Stir in applesauce and vanilla.

In a separate bowl, sift together all the dry ingredients before stirring them into the mixture. Add the raisins, Calvados, and pecans, stirring until just combined.

Pour the batter into the prepared pan. Bake 45 to 50 minutes, until a skewer inserted in the middle comes out clean.

Leave the cake in the pan on a rack to cool to room temperature before inverting onto a serving plate.

CHOCOLATE ROLL CAKE WITH STRAWBERRY FOOL

No simpler dessert exists! Garnish the top with picture-perfect strawberries and a few chocolate curls.

4 eggs, separated
¾ cup granulated sugar
½ teaspoon vanilla extract

½ cup all-purpose flour
⅓ cup unsweetened cocoa powder
1 teaspoon baking powder

½ quantity Strawberry Fool (see page 38)
Large block bittersweet chocolate, for decorating

Heat the oven to 350°F. Lightly grease an 15½ x 10½-inch jelly-roll pan. Line the bottom and sides with baking parchment; butter and flour the paper.

Place the egg yolks in a bowl and beat with an electric mixer until they begin to thicken. Add the sugar and continue to beat until very thick and pale yellow, about 7 minutes. Stir in the vanilla.

In a separate bowl, sift the flour, cocoa, and baking powder. Gradually fold in the dry ingredients. Spread the batter in the prepared pan and smooth the surface.

Bake in the middle of the oven 12 to 15 minutes, until springy in the middle. Leave the cake to cool completely in the pan on a wire rack.

Meanwhile, sprinkle a clean dish towel with confectioners' sugar. Immediately invert the cake onto the towel and peel off the paper. Cover the cake with strawberry fool and gently roll up the cake with the help of the towel. Place it on a serving plate. Refrigerate at least 6 hours before serving.

To decorate, chill the block of chocolate and use a vegetable peeler to shave off curls. Dust the top of the cake with confectioners' sugar, then pile on the curls just before serving.

PEAR TART

Make sure you also try this custard-based tart with your favorite apple. It's easy to make and quick to disappear.

½ quantity Classic Pie and Tart Crust
(see page 61), baked in a 9-inch tart pan
with a removable bottom
3 large ripe pears, peeled, cored, and
thinly sliced

⅔ cup heavy cream
¼ cup + 1 tablespoon granulated sugar
2 eggs
1 teaspoon vanilla extract
1 tablespoon dark rum

Heat the oven to 350°F.

Leave the tart shell in the pan and arrange the pear slices decoratively over the bottom. Beat together the remaining ingredients except the 1 tablespoon of sugar, to make the custard. Pour it over the pears.

Bake the tart in the middle of the oven 35 to 40 minutes, until the custard is set. If desired, sprinkle the remaining sugar over the tart and place it under a hot broiler for a few minutes to glaze.

APPLE–PEAR PIE

A classic American favorite. Dress up this dessert with a lattice topping or just have a simple "lid." Either way, serve it with vanilla ice cream!

1 quantity Classic Pie and Tart Crust
(see page 61), unbaked
2 pounds apples, peeled, cored, and
cut into ¼-inch slices
1 pound pears, peeled, cored, and
cut into ½-inch slices

2 tablespoons all-purpose flour
2 teaspoons ground cinnamon
2 teaspoons fresh lemon juice
1 teaspoon vanilla extract
1 egg, beaten with 1 tablespoon water

Heat the oven to 375°F. Adjust the shelf to the lowest level in the oven. Roll out half of the dough and line a 9-inch pie plate; set aside. Roll out the remaining dough to about ⅛ inch thick and cut it into lattice strips (see page 61).

Toss all the remaining ingredients together, except the beaten egg, and pile them into the pie plate. Arrange the lattice strips across the top and crimp the edges. Using a thin pastry brush, brush the lattice strips with the beaten egg.

Bake 50 to 60 minutes, until the pastry is golden and the apples are tender if you pierce then with a skewer through the lattice.

BLOOD ORANGE TART

Blood oranges are one of nature's most glamorous fruits. Their season is short, so dramatize them when available. The candied slices in this recipe are also wonderful served alone or as a striking decoration for other desserts. Don't forget, however, to allow enough time to make them the day before you plan to serve this.

1 cup granulated sugar
⅔ cup water
2 tablespoons light corn syrup
½ vanilla bean, split
3 or 4 medium blood oranges, sliced
⅛ inch thick

1 quantity Sweet Tart Pastry (see
page 60), baked in a 9-inch fluted
tart pan with a removable bottom
1½ cups Pastry Cream (see page 58)

Combine the sugar, water, corn syrup, and vanilla bean in a large skillet. Bring to a boil, stirring to dissolve the sugar. Reduce the heat and add the orange slices. Simmer 10 minutes, swirling the pan occasionally. Remove the pan from the heat and leave it to sit until the orange slices and syrup are cool. Remove the slices from the syrup and place them on a rack over a dish to dry. Refrigerate overnight.

Meanwhile, reduce the syrup until very thick and refrigerate as well.

The next day, fill the tart shell with the pastry cream and arrange the orange slices, slightly overlapping, to cover the cream. Gently reheat the syrup and brush this over the tart as a glaze.

Right: Chocolate Roll Cake with Strawberry Fool

VIRGINIA SPONGE CAKE WITH FRESH CHERRIES

This is one of the most versatile cakes around! It can be frosted with whipped cream and served with berries, or sliced for summer puddings. Here it is flavored with lemon and served with Cherry Compote. Serves 8 to 10.

FOR THE CAKE:

6 eggs, separated	*¼ teaspoon cream of tartar*
3 tablespoons lemon juice, or 2 teaspoons vanilla extract	*1⅓ cups cake flour, sifted twice*
2 teaspoons grated lemon peel (optional)	*¼ teaspoon salt*
1¼ cups granulated sugar	

FOR THE CHERRY COMPOTE:

1 pound Bing cherries, pitted	*⅔ cup granulated sugar*
1 pound White Rainier cherries, pitted	*2 tablespoons brandy*

Heat the oven to 350°F. Line the bottom of a 10-inch tube pan with baking parchment.

Beat the egg yolks, lemon juice, grated peel, and 1 cup of the sugar until thick and fluffy.

Beat the egg whites with the cream of tartar and salt until soft peaks form. Gradually add the sugar and continue beating until stiff and glossy.

Fold one-third of the whites into the yolks to lighten the batter. Alternately fold in the remaining whites and the flour.

Pour the batter into the prepared pan. Bake in the middle of the oven 50 minutes, until golden brown and the cake springs to the touch. Cool completely before removing from pan.

For the compote, combine all ingredients; set aside at least 2 hours, stirring occasionally.

To serve, cut slices with a serrated knife and garnish with the cherries.

PLUM GALETTE

Black Beauty plums are plump and juicy, perfect for this rustic dessert.

1 quantity Galette Dough (see page 61)	*2 tablespoons all-purpose flour*
2¼ pounds ripe plums	*1 teaspoon vanilla extract*
½ cup granulated sugar	*1 tablespoon lemon juice*
¼ teaspoon ground nutmeg	*Sugar cubes, for garnish*

Heat the oven to 400°F. Line a baking sheet with parchment paper.

Roll out the galette dough into a 12-inch circle. Transfer to the baking sheet.

In a large bowl, combine all the other ingredients. Pile this filling into the middle of the dough, spreading it to about 2 inches from the edge. Fold the edge over the filling, pleating the dough and pressing it to seal. Coarsely crush the sugar cubes and press around the edge of the dough.

Bake in the middle of the oven about 50 minutes, until the fruit is tender and the crust browned.

KEY LIME CHIFFON PIE

Key limes are plentiful in the southern states, and the juice is sold bottled. If you can't find Key limes or their juice, use ordinary limes instead. Be sure to prepare the pretzel crust before you begin the filling so it has plenty of time to chill and set.

1 tablespoon unflavored gelatin	*5 egg whites*
¼ cup water	*3 tablespoons granulated sugar*
1 quantity Lemon Curd (see page 58), made with Key lime juice instead of lemon juice	*½ cup heavy cream, whipped*
	1 quantity Pretzel Crust (see page 60), prepared in a 9-inch pie plate

TO DECORATE:
Whipped cream and pretzels

Dissolve the gelatin in the water. Either prepare the Key lime curd now and leave it in the saucepan, or return the prepared curd to a saucepan and heat it gently. Stir in the gelatin until it is dissolved. Remove the pan from the heat and transfer the curd mixture to a bowl to cool to room temperature, stirring frequently.

When the curd has cooled and thickened, place the egg whites into a separate bowl and beat until soft peaks form. Gradually add the sugar and continue beating until glossy. Fold the curd into the whites along with the whipped cream.

Pour the mixture into the pastry shell. Chill for at least 4 hours before serving. Garnish the pie with whipped cream and pretzels.

Right: Plum Galette

BLACKBERRY–RHUBARB PIE

Every time my friend Ann Mileti makes this pie, the neighborhood is quickly on her doorstep. There is no mistaking the aroma of this freshly baked treat. I always lay a couple of pieces of foil underneath the pie to catch any drippings.

½ quantity Classic Pie and Tart Crust (see page 61), unbaked
1¼ pounds rhubarb, trimmed and cut into 1-inch pieces
1⅓ cups granulated sugar

⅓ cup cornstarch
3 tablespoons water
3 cups (1 pound) blackberries, rinsed
1 egg yolk
1 tablespoon heavy cream

Heat the oven to 375°F. Adjust the shelf to the lowest level in the oven. Roll out half of the dough and line a 9-inch pie plate; set aside. Roll out the remaining dough about ⅛ inch thick and cut out lattice strips (see page 61).

In a large saucepan, combine the rhubarb and sugar and simmer over medium-low heat 5 minutes, until the rhubarb is just tender but not falling apart.

In a small bowl, stir the cornstarch and water to make a smooth paste. Stir the paste into the rhubarb mixture and cook, stirring constantly, until thickened and boiling. Remove the pan from the heat and stir in the blackberries.

Spoon the filling into the pie plate. Arrange the lattice strips across the top and crimp the edges. Beat together the egg yolk and cream and brush over the lattice.

Bake about 50 minutes, until the top is golden brown.

MILE–HIGH LEMON MERINGUE PIE

The tart and tangy curd filling is the perfect foil for the billows of meringue topping. The secret to a "no-weep" meringue is two-fold: one, always top with meringue while the curd is still hot, and two, always make sure the meringue touches the edges of the crust. This way the meringue cooks on the bottom from the hot curd and sticks to the edges to prevent shrinking.

2 quantities Lemon Curd (see page 58)
½ quantity Classic Pie and Tart Crust (see page 61), baked in a 9-inch tart pan with a removable bottom

5 egg whites
3 tablespoons granulated sugar

Heat the oven to 375°F. Pour the hot lemon curd into the pastry shell; set aside.

Beat the egg whites until soft peaks form. Gradually add the sugar and continue beating until stiff and glossy. Pile the meringue onto the warm curd, making sure it reaches the edge of the pastry. Swirl the top decoratively.

Bake in the middle of the oven 20 to 25 minutes, until the meringue is brown and puffed.

MRS. BELL'S RHUBARB CUSTARD PIE

In this recipe the rhubarb caramelizes while the pie bakes, providing a nice contrast to the custard. If time is short, skip the lattice work and top it with decorative dough cut-outs instead.

1 quantity Classic Pie and Tart Crust (see page 61), unbaked
1 pound rhubarb, coarsely chopped
1⅓ cups granulated sugar

2 eggs
3 tablespoons all-purpose flour
1 tablespoon unsalted butter, melted
¼ teaspoon ground nutmeg

FOR THE EGG WASH:
1 egg
1 tablespoon light cream

Heat the oven to 450°F. Adjust the shelf to the lowest level in the oven.

Roll out half the dough and line a 9-inch pie plate; set aside. Roll out the remaining pastry to about ⅛ inch thick and cut into lattice strips (see page 61).

Pile the rhubarb into the pie plate. Beat together the sugar, eggs, flour, butter, and nutmeg until smooth. Pour this custard mixture over the rhubarb. Arrange the lattice strips across the top and crimp the edges. Beat together the remaining egg and the cream and brush over the lattice.

Bake the pie 10 minutes. Reduce the temperature to 350°F and bake 30 minutes longer, or until a knife inserted near the middle comes out clean.

PLUM–ALMOND TART

A ripe plum or apricot is the jewel in any frangipani tart. Make sure you try both versions of this recipe!

⅓ cup granulated sugar
¾ cup sliced almonds, toasted
¼ cup unsalted butter, at room temperature
1 egg

1 teaspoon vanilla extract
1 quantity Sweet Tart Pastry (see page 60), baked in a 9-inch tart pan
3 or 4 ripe, firm plums, cut into ½ inch slices

Heat the oven to 375°F.

In a food processor, combine the sugar and almonds and pulse until well ground. Add the butter and process until smooth. Add the egg and vanilla and process until just combined. Spread this almond filling into the tart shell. Arrange the fruit decoratively on top.

Bake in the middle of the oven 40 to 45 minutes, until the fruit is tender and the filling is light brown.

APRICOT VARIATION:
Substitute apricot slices for the plums and add a pinch of cinnamon to the almond filling. Proceed as directed above.

Right: Blackberry–Rhubarb Pie

LEMON CURD TART

Any spring or summer fruit will be beautiful atop this delicious tart.

1 quantity Lemon Curd (see page 58)
½ quantity Classic Pie and Tart Crust
(see page 61), baked in a 9-inch tart pan
with a removable bottom

2½ cups (1 pound) strawberries, hulled
if large, rinsed, and dried
Confectioners' sugar and lemon peel,
to decorate

Spread the lemon curd into the pastry shell. Cut thin strips of lemon peel and arrange in crisscrosses on top. Arrange the strawberries decoratively on the top. Sprinkle with confectioners' sugar.

FRUIT TORTE

Super fast and super easy, this versatile little cake accommodates many different fruits and occasions.

½ cup unsalted butter, at room
temperature
¾ cup + 1 tablespoon granulated sugar
2 eggs
½ teaspoon vanilla extract

1½ cups all-purpose flour

1 teaspoon baking powder
¼ teaspoon salt
½ cup milk
1 cup (about 4 ounces) raspberries,
blueberries, or blackberries, or 2 plums or 1
peach, thinly sliced

Heat the oven to 350°F. Lightly grease and flour an 8-inch square cake pan, 2 inches deep.

Beat the butter and ¾ cup of the sugar until light and fluffy. Stir in the eggs and vanilla.

In a separate bowl, combine the dry ingredients. Alternately add the milk and dry ingredients to the butter mixture until just blended. Spoon the batter into the prepared pan.

Arrange the berries or sliced fruit on the top and sprinkle with the remaining sugar. Bake in the middle of the oven 45 minutes, until golden and a skewer inserted in the middle comes out clean.

FRUITY UPSIDE–DOWN CAKE

Vary the fruited topping according to what fruits are in season. This should serve 4 to 6.

FOR THE CAKE:
1 quantity Fruit Torte Cake batter
(see left), omitting the fruit and only
using ½ cup sugar
2 or 3 plums, sliced, or 14 ounces cherries,
pitted and halved

FOR THE CARAMEL:
½ cup granulated sugar
¼ cup water

Heat the oven to 350°F. Lightly grease an 8-inch square cake pan, 2 inches deep.

Prepare the caramel according to directions in Coconut Crème Caramel (see page 41). Pour the caramel into the prepared pan and let it stand 5 minutes to set. Arrange the fruit decoratively on top of the caramel; set aside.

Prepare the fruit torte cake batter according to the directions, using only ½ cup sugar. Spoon the batter evenly over the fruit in the pan.

Bake the cake in the middle of the oven 45 minutes, or until golden and a skewer inserted in the middle comes out clean. Immediately invert the pan onto a serving dish, allowing the caramel to drip down the sides.

APRICOT CHEESECAKE

Sulfured apricots retain their bright orange color and give this cheesecake a distinctive look. This recipe should serve about 8.

1½ cups vanilla cookie crumbs,
finely crushed
½ cup unsalted butter, melted
1 tablespoon grated orange peel
6 ounces dried apricots
1 tablespoon orange-flavored liqueur

1½ pounds cream cheese, at room
temperature
¾ cup granulated sugar
4 eggs
½ cup sour cream
1 teaspoon vanilla extract

Heat the oven to 325°F. Lightly grease a 9-inch springform pan.

Combine the crumbs, butter, and orange peel. Press into the bottom and about 1 inch up the side of the pan.

Cover the apricots with water and simmer 20 minutes, until very tender. Drain them well and finely chop them before tossing with the liqueur; set aside.

Beat the cream cheese until very smooth. Add sugar and continue beating until fluffy. Add the eggs, one at a time. Stir in the apricots, sour cream, and vanilla. Spoon the batter into the pan.

Bake in a water bath 1 hour, until the top is firm to the touch and the cake jiggles slightly. Leave to cool to room temperature before removing from the pan.

Right: Lemon Curd Tart

PUDDINGS, CUSTARDS, TEATIME TREATS

Many of these recipes can be served as a dessert to follow a meal or as an afternoon pick-me-up served with a cup of tea. Thanks to the fruit, they are soothing and satisfying with just the right touch of richness. All recipes serve 4 to 6 unless stated otherwise.

RICE PUDDING WITH DRIED CHERRIES

Creamy, rich rice pudding made the old-fashioned way. When serving the pudding chilled, stir in some milk or cream to lighten it.

2 cups milk	*Pinch of salt*
2 cups light cream	*⅔ cup dried cherries*
4 strips of orange peel	*1 teaspoon vanilla extract*
⅓ cup short-grain white rice	*¼ to ½ cup milk or heavy cream*
⅓ cup granulated sugar	*(optional)*

Combine the milk, light cream, and orange peel in a saucepan. Bring it to a boil, then slowly stir in the rice. Reduce the heat and simmer about 35 minutes, stirring frequently, until the rice is very tender. Stir in the sugar, salt, and cherries. Cook 15 minutes longer, until the cherries are tender. Stir in the vanilla.

Serve warm or chilled, adding the milk or heavy cream if the pudding is chilled.

BLUEBERRY CORNBREAD

Serve these wedges at an afternoon brunch or a southwestern-style dinner party.

1 cup coarse yellow cornmeal	*¾ cup buttermilk*
1 cup all-purpose flour	*1 egg*
½ cup granulated sugar	*⅔ cup unsalted butter, melted*
2½ teaspoons baking powder	*and cooled*
¼ teaspoon salt	*1 cup (5 ounces) blueberries, lightly mashed*

Heat the oven to 375°F. Grease a 9-inch pie plate.
Combine the cornmeal, flour, sugar, baking powder, and salt in a medium bowl. In another bowl, mix together the remaining ingredients. Pour the wet ingredients into the dry and mix them gently to combine. Spread the batter in the pie plate.

Bake in the middle of the oven about 35 minutes, until golden brown and the middle springs back when touched.

STRAWBERRY SHORTCAKE WITH RHUBARB FOOL

The essential summer dessert! Substitute Strawberry Fool (see page 38) for the rhubarb for an extra-strawberry treat. Serves 6.

2 cups (12 ounces) sliced strawberries	*1 quantity Shortcakes (see page 60),*
2 tablespoons granulated sugar	*baked in a 9-inch circle (it should*
1 tablespoon fresh lemon juice	*take about 25 minutes), cooled*
	1 quantity Rhubarb Fool (see page 41)

Toss the strawberries with the sugar and the lemon juice. Chill for at least 1 hour, stirring occasionally.

Just before serving, gently slice the shortcake in half horizontally. Place the bottom half on a serving plate and spread about two-thirds of the rhubarb fool over the layer. Spoon half the fruit and juices on top of the fool. Top with the remaining shortcake layer. Dollop the fool on top and garnish with the remaining strawberries and juices.

BLACKBERRY PUDDING

Sprinkle the bread slices with 2 or 3 tablespoons of sherry just before adding the hot berries to make the alcohol flavor more prominent.

10 slices thin stale white bread, no crusts
6 cups (30 ounces) blackberries
1 to 1½ cups granulated sugar

3 tablespoons fresh lemon juice
1 tablespoon grated lemon peel
3 tablespoons very dry sherry (optional)

Line a 1-quart bowl with the bread slices (reserving some slices for the topping), slightly overlapping to cover any holes.

Combine the blackberries, sugar, and lemon juice and peel in a saucepan and simmer until the sugar dissolves and the berries are tender and juicy. Sprinkle the bread with the sherry, if using. Spoon the hot berries into the bread-lined bowl and top with the remaining bread, cut to fit.

Cover the pudding with plastic wrap and top with a plate or cardboard. Place a 1-pound weight on top and refrigerate the pudding for at least 10 hours.

Below: *Classic Cherry Clafouti*

CITRUS CRISP COOKIES

This refreshing, light snap cookie can also be made into small cups to hold sorbets or firm mousses. To do this, spread the batter to the desired size and bake. Remove the cookies from the baking sheet immediately and mold each one on an upside-down custard cup. Leave until cool and firm, then remove. These will keep for up to a week in an airtight container. Makes 3 dozen.

1½ cups all-purpose flour
½ teaspoon salt
1½ teaspoons grated citrus peel, such as lime, orange, or lemon—any combination is nice
1½ sticks (¾ cup) unsalted butter, at room temperature

1¼ cups granulated sugar
2 large eggs
1¼ teaspoons lemon extract

Heat the oven to 350°F. Line 2 baking sheets with parchment paper.

Sift together the flour and salt, then stir in the peel. Beat the butter and sugar together until light and fluffy. Add the eggs, one at a time. Stir in the lemon extract before folding in the dry ingredients.

Pipe or drop tablespoonfuls of the dough 2 inches apart onto the baking sheets.

Bake 8 to10 minutes, until golden around the edges. Remove the cookies from the baking sheets and place on a rack to cool completely.

CLASSIC CHERRY CLAFOUTI

Nothing beats the classic version of this pudding dessert—except maybe the peach variation below.

⅓ cup + 2 tablespoons granulated sugar
12 ounces Bing cherries, stems and pits removed
½ cup all-purpose flour
Pinch of salt

¼ cup sour cream
3 large eggs
1 cup milk
1 teaspoon vanilla extract
1 tablespoon unsalted butter, at room temperature

Heat the oven to 375°F. Grease a shallow 9-inch baking dish and sprinkle it with 1 tablespoon of the sugar. Arrange the cherries over the bottom.

Sift together the flour, ⅓ cup sugar, and salt. Stir together the sour cream, eggs, milk, and vanilla. Whisk these ingredients into the dry ingredients until smooth.

Pour the batter over the fruit. Dot the pudding with the butter and sprinkle with the remaining 1 tablespoon sugar. Bake 40 to 45 minutes, until puffed and brown. Serve warm.

PEACH–ALMOND VARIATION:
Cut 1 pound ripe peaches into ½-inch slices and toss with 2 tablespoons granulated sugar, 1 tablespoon all-purpose flour, and ¼ teaspoon almond extract. Arrange the fruit on the bottom of a dish prepared as above. Pour the batter over the fruit and top the pudding with ⅓ cup sliced almonds. Bake as above.

SHORTCAKES WITH CARAMELIZED PEARS AND GINGER CREAM

Who says shortcake is just for the summertime? Caramelized pears and ginger cream lend a warm earthy feel to the traditional shortcake. This recipe makes 8.

*1 quantity Shortcakes (see page 60),
baked and cooled*

FOR THE PEARS:
¼ cup unsalted butter
*4 firm, ripe pears, peeled, cored, and cut
into ½-inch slices*
⅓ cup granulated sugar
¼ teaspoon fresh lemon juice

FOR THE GINGER CREAM:
1½ cups heavy cream
¼ cup granulated sugar
2 teaspoons vanilla extract
½ teaspoon ground ginger

To caramelize the pears, melt the butter in a large skillet over medium-low heat. Arrange the pears in the pan so they barely overlap and sprinkle them with the sugar and lemon juice. Sauté the slices, turning them regularly, 20 to 25 minutes, until caramelized. Remove from the heat and keep at room temperature.

Whip the cream, gradually adding the sugar, until semi-firm peaks form. Stir in the vanilla and ginger.

To serve, separate the shortcakes in half and layer them with the pears and cream.

CRANBERRY SCONES

A cheery alternative to the original scone. Dried currants can easily be substituted for the cranberries. This recipe makes 6.

⅓ cup dried cranberries
⅓ cup fresh orange juice
2 cups all-purpose flour
2 teaspoons baking powder
¼ teaspoon salt

¼ cup granulated sugar
*1 stick (½ cup) unsalted butter,
chilled and diced*
¾ cup buttermilk

Heat the oven to 400°F. Line a baking sheet with parchment paper.

Combine the cranberries and orange juice in a saucepan and bring to a simmer. Remove from the heat; let sit for 15 minutes.

Meanwhile, in a bowl, combine the flour, baking powder, salt, and 3 tablespoons of the sugar. Cut in the butter until coarse crumbs form. Drain the cranberries, reserving the liquid, and add them with the buttermilk to the crumbs, tossing gently to combine.

Shape the scone dough into a flat 8-inch circle. Cut this into 6 triangles. Brush with the reserved juice and sprinkle with the remaining sugar. Bake on the baking sheet 18 minutes, or until puffed and golden brown. Serve straight from the oven or at room temperature.

Above: Mango–Raspberry Shortcakes

MANGO–RASPBERRY SHORTCAKES

To get clean slices of mango, refer to the instructions given in "Helpful Hints for Handling Fruit" (see page 10). This recipe makes 8 scrumptious shortcakes.

2 ripe mangoes, sliced
1 pint raspberries
¼ cup granulated sugar
1 teaspoon grated lime peel
1 to 2 tablespoons orange-flavored liqueur
1 teaspoon vanilla extract

2 cups heavy cream
*1 quantity Shortcakes (see page
60), with ½ teaspoon ground nutmeg
added to the dry ingredients, cut into eight
3-inch circles, and baked*

Combine the mangoes and raspberries with the sugar, lime peel, and liqueur. Toss everything together and set aside for at least 1 hour.

Just before serving, add the vanilla to the cream and whip until soft peaks form. Split the shortcakes in half and layer them with the whipped cream and fruit. Serve at once.

Peach cobbler

Summer peaches are never more delicious than when tossed with a bit of sugar and topped with a light and puffy buttermilk crust.

FILLING:

3 pounds ripe peaches, cut into	*1 tablespoon fresh lemon juice*
½-inch slices	*2 tablespoons all-purpose flour*
¼ to ½ cup granulated sugar	
(amount depends on sweetness of peaches)	

TOPPING:

1½ cups all-purpose flour	*1 large egg, beaten*
½ cup granulated sugar	*⅔ cup buttermilk*
2½ teaspoons baking powder	*6 tablespoons unsalted butter, melted*
¼ teaspoon salt	*and cooled*

Heat the oven to 375°F. Lightly grease a 2- to 2½-quart baking dish. In a large bowl, toss all the filling ingredients together, then spoon them into the prepared dish.

To make the topping, combine the flour, sugar, baking powder, and salt in a medium bowl. Add the remaining ingredients and toss gently to blend into a dough. Drop heaped spoonfuls of the mixture onto the fruit to cover.

Bake the cobbler in the middle of the oven 40 minutes, until it is golden brown on top and the filling is bubbly.

Banana waffles

These waffles freeze beautifully. Layer them with foil and freeze them for up to three months. Reheat them under the broiler. They're delicious topped with whipped cream and sliced bananas. Makes about 8 waffles.

2 cups all-purpose flour	*½ cup sour cream*
3 tablespoons granulated sugar	*1¼ cups milk*
2½ teaspoons baking powder	*1 stick (½ cup) butter, melted*
¾ teaspoon baking soda	*⅓ cup canola oil*
¾ teaspoon salt	*1 teaspoon vanilla extract*
4 large eggs, separated	*½ cup chopped toasted walnuts*
¾ cup mashed ripe banana	*(optional)*

Heat a waffle iron according to the manufacturer's directions. Sift the flour, sugar, baking powder, baking soda, and salt together. In a separate bowl, beat the egg yolks and all the remaining ingredients, except the egg whites and nuts, until well blended. Stir in the dry ingredients until just blended.

Beat the egg whites until stiff but not dry. Fold the whites and nuts, if using, into the batter.

Cook according to the waffle manufacturer's directions.

Raspberry drop muffins

Although these aren't really muffins, the texture is soft and cakelike, similar to that of a classic muffin. Regardless of the name, however, try them with your favorite berry! This recipe makes 8.

1 cup all-purpose flour	*4 tablespoons unsalted butter, chilled and*
⅓ cup granulated sugar	*diced*
1½ teaspoons baking powder	*½ cup sour cream*
Pinch of salt	*½ cup (2 ounces) raspberries*

Heat the oven to 375°F. Lightly grease a baking sheet or line it with parchment paper.

Combine the flour, sugar, baking powder, and salt in a medium bowl. Cut in the butter until coarse crumbs form. Stir in the sour cream and raspberries until just combined. The dough will be sticky! Drop 8 mounds onto the baking sheet.

Bake the muffins in the middle of the oven 20 to 25 minutes, until puffed, springy, and golden brown.

Red berry pudding

Thick slices of stale sponge cake are delicious with this berry mix. Stale bread also works well.

14 thick slices stale Virginia	*1 cup granulated sugar*
Sponge Cake (see page 24)	*¼ cup orange-flavored liqueur*
1¼ pounds mixed red berries,	*2 teaspoons grated lemon peel*
such as raspberries, strawberries,	
and red currants	

Line a 1½-quart bowl or soufflé dish with the cake slices, filling in any holes, but reserving some of the slices to top the pudding.

Hull and quarter the strawberries. Combine all the ingredients and simmer until the sugar dissolves and the fruit is tender and juicy. Spoon the mixture into the dish and top with the remaining cake slices.

Cover the pudding with plastic wrap and top with a plate. Place a 1-pound weight on the top and refrigerate for at least 10 hours.

Right: Peach Cobbler

BLUEBERRY QUEEN OF PUDDINGS

Taste this little-known dessert gem and be ready to fall in love! The traditional version calls for jam, but nothing beats the taste of fresh blueberries. This should serve 6 to 8.

2 slices stale white bread	*2 teaspoons grated lemon peel*
2¼ cups milk	*2 tablespoons all-purpose flour*
1 cup granulated sugar	*3 tablespoons fresh lemon juice*
4 egg yolks	*3 egg whites*
¼ teaspoon vanilla extract	*3 tablespoons granulated sugar*
1½ cups (8 ounces) blueberries	

Heat the oven to 350°F. Grease an 8-inch square baking dish.

Crumble the bread slices and layer these in the dish. Combine the milk, ½ cup sugar, the egg yolks, and vanilla. Pour this over the bread; let stand 15 minutes for the bread to swell.

Bake the pudding in the middle of the oven 30 minutes, until custard is almost set.

Meanwhile, combine blueberries, another ½ cup sugar, the lemon peel, and the flour in a small saucepan. Stir in the lemon juice. Bring to a simmer and simmer about 15 minutes, stirring constantly, until the berries are tender and the liquid is thick. When the custard is baked, carefully spread the blueberries over the top.

Beat the egg whites until soft peaks form. Gradually add the remaining sugar and continue beating until glossy. Spoon this over the blueberries and bake 25 minutes longer, or until the meringue is puffed and brown.

INDIVIDUAL BLUEBERRY SUMMER PUDDINGS

Thinly sliced bread works best with individual puddings. The fruit is the true star of this dessert. This recipe makes 6.

About 20 thin slices of stale white bread	*1½ teaspoons ground cinnamon*
6 cups (30 ounces) blueberries	*2 tablespoons dry sherry (optional)*
1½ cups granulated sugar	*Whipped cream, to decorate*

Line 6 ramekins with the bread, reserving some for the topping. Make sure there are no holes.

Over low heat, simmer together all the other ingredients until the sugar dissolves and the fruit is tender and juicy. Spoon the mixture into the ramekins and top them with the remaining bread, cut to fit. Cover them with plastic wrap and weight each one down. Refrigerate for at least 10 hours.

To serve, invert the puddings and decorate them with whipped cream, if desired.

INDIAN PUDDINGS

A favorite American comfort food. Experiment with different types of dried fruits, or just go with raisins. This recipe makes 8.

1 quart milk	*2 eggs*
¼ cup molasses	*¾ cup coarse yellow cornmeal*
⅓ cup packed light brown sugar	*½ cup dried fruit*

Heat the oven to 325°F. Lightly butter 8 ramekins.

Combine the milk, molasses, sugar, and eggs in a large saucepan. Whisk them over medium heat about 3 minutes, until slightly thickened. Gradually whisk in the cornmeal. Simmer, stirring constantly, until the mixture is bubbly and thick.

Spoon the batter into the prepared ramekins and top with the dried fruit. Bake the puddings in a water bath about 60 minutes, until set. Serve warm or chilled.

Right: Individual Blueberry Summer Puddings

MOUSSES, SOUFFLÉS, SABAYONS

Here is a selection of light and airy desserts. Most of the fluffiness comes from the addition of beaten egg whites or cream, or both, and the addition of fruit keeps things fresh tasting. All recipes serve 4 to 6 unless stated otherwise.

RED CURRANT SOUFFLÉ

For variety, substitute raspberries for half of the red currants, reducing the quantity of sugar to about ¾ cup and strain the purée before folding it into the egg whites.

2 cups (10 ounces) red currants	*6 egg whites,*
1 tablespoon Grand Marnier or	*Pinch of salt*
similar liqueur	*Confectioners' sugar, to decorate*
1 to 1¼ cup granulated sugar	

Heat the oven to 375°F. Grease and sugar a 1-quart soufflé dish.

Combine the red currants, reserving a few for the decoration, Grand Marnier, and all but ⅓ cup of the sugar in a saucepan. Simmer, stirring constantly, until the currants are juicy and the sugar dissolves. Strain and chill thoroughly.

Beat the egg whites and salt until soft peaks form. Continue beating and gradually add the remaining sugar until stiff and glossy. Gently fold the cold purée into the egg whites until well blended. Spoon into the prepared dish.

Bake in the middle of the oven 30 minutes, until puffed and browned. Decorate with confectioners' sugar and fresh currants. Serve immediately.

BERRY GRATINS

Any combination of fresh, sweet summer berries will be delicious and elegant when topped with a rich sabayon. Don't forget, the sabayon must be whipped up at the last minute. This recipe makes 6.

4 cups (about 1 pound) mixed fresh berries	*2 tablespoons Marsala wine, sherry, brandy,*
(hull and quarter strawberries if using)	*or rum*
½ cup granulated sugar	*3 large eggs*
Pinch of salt	

Divide the berries into 6 shallow flameproof serving dishes. Heat the broiler to medium-high.

Combine the remaining ingredients in a bowl. Set the bowl over simmering water and whisk constantly about 3 minutes, until the sabayon is very thick and creamy.

Spoon over the berries. Set the dishes on a baking sheet. Place under the broiler 3 to 4 minutes, until golden brown. Serve immediately.

APRICOT MOUSSES

Fresh, ripe apricots are essential to this delicate, flavorsome mousse. Decorate with apricot slices and dessert cookies. Serves 4.

1 envelope unflavored gelatin	*2 tablespoons fresh lemon juice*
¼ cup fresh orange juice	*2 egg whites, beaten until stiff*
¾ cup apricot purée	*⅔ cup heavy cream, whipped*
⅓ cup granulated sugar	

Mix the gelatin with the orange juice. In a saucepan, combine the apricot purée, sugar, and lemon juice. Simmer, stirring, to dissolve the sugar. Add the dissolved gelatin and stir. Cool the mixture to room temperature, when it should be thickened but not set.

Fold in the egg whites and cream. Spoon into serving goblets. Chill for at least 6 hours before serving.

CHOCOLATE SABAYON WITH BLOOD ORANGES

This is one fast dessert! While blood oranges are delicious and beautiful, their season is short. Pineapple makes a terrific substitute.

3 blood oranges, sectioned with all the	*½ cup granulated sugar*
pith removed	*3 tablespoons brandy*
4 large eggs	*4 ounces bittersweet chocolate, chopped*

Arrange the orange sections on a serving plate; set aside. In a medium bowl, combine the eggs, sugar, and brandy. Set the bowl over simmering water and beat about 5 mintutes, until thickened. Remove the bowl from the heat and beat in the chocolate until smooth. Spoon the sabayon over the oranges and serve immediately.

STRAWBERRY FOOL

Feel free to use any combination of red berries for this super-simple, super-rich dessert. For a stylish presentation, serve in Citrus Crisp Cookie cups (see page 32) and decorate with a few whole berries.

12 ounces strawberries, hulled and halved	*½ teaspoon vanilla extract*
¼ cup granulated sugar	*1¼ cups heavy cream*

Mash the strawberries, reserving a few for decoration, with the sugar until juicy and coarse. Refrigerate until very cold, then stir in the vanilla.

Whip the cream until stiff, then fold in the strawberry mixture. Transfer to a serving dish and refrigerate at least 4 hours, until firmer, before serving.

Above: *Pear Charlotte*

BLACK CURRANT MOUSSES

The distinctive color of the black currants gives these individual mousses a striking appearance. Serves 4.

2 teaspoons unflavored gelatin	*1 cup granulated sugar*
¼ cup + 3 tablespoons water	*2 large egg whites*
1 pound black currants, removed from	*1 cup heavy cream, whipped*
stems	

Dissolve the gelatin in 3 tablespoons of the water. Combine the black currants, ¼ cup water, and all but 2 tablespoons of the sugar in a saucepan. Simmer, stirring constantly, until the fruit is soft.

Remove the pan from the heat and stir in the gelatin. Strain the mixture into a large bowl; set it aside to cool to the consistency of unbeaten egg whites.

In a separate bowl, whisk the egg whites until soft peaks form. Continue whisking while gradually adding the remaining sugar until the mixture is stiff and glossy. Fold the whites and whipped cream into the chilled purée. Pour into serving glasses and chill.

MOUSSE CAKE VARIATION:
Slice a baked Genoise Sponge (see page 58) in half and place it in a 9-inch springform pan. Sprinkle this with 2 tablespoons Grand Marnier. Pour half of the mousse into the pan and layer it with thinly sliced kiwi fruit. Pour in the remaining mousse mixture and chill until set.

PEAR CHARLOTTE

Sophisticated and elegant, this dessert is also surprisingly easy to prepare. If you're short of time, tinned pear halves in a light syrup can easily replace home-poached. Serves 6 to 8.

1 envelope unflavored gelatin	*½ cup milk*
2 tablespoons water	*3 egg yolks*
4 tablespoons pear-flavored liqueur	*¼ cup + 1 tablespoon granulated sugar*
2 or 3 pears, poached, halved and drained	*2 egg whites*
with ½ cup of the liquid reserved	*¾ cup heavy cream, whipped*
1 layer vanilla-flavored Genoise Sponge	*½ ounce bittersweet chocolate, melted,*
(see page 58), ½ inch thick	*to decorate (optional)*

Dissolve the gelatin in the water and half of the liqueur. Cut the pear halves into ½-inch thick slices. Reserve 8 of the slices and chop the remaining ones into smaller pieces.

Place the Genoise layer in the bottom of a 9-inch springform pan. Sprinkle it with the remaining liqueur and the smaller pieces of pear.

In a saucepan, combine the pear poaching liquid with the milk and bring it to a simmer.

Meanwhile, whisk together the egg yolks and ¼ cup sugar and slowly add the hot liquid. Return the mixture to the pan over medium heat, stirring constantly, until thick enough to coat the back of a spoon. Stir in the gelatin until completely dissolved before allowing the mixture to cool.

In a separate bowl, whisk the egg whites until soft peaks form. Add the 1 tablespoon sugar and beat until glossy. Fold the egg whites and whipped cream into the cooled custard. Pour it into the cake tin and refrigerate at least 6 hours until set.

To serve, remove the pan. Decorate with the remaining pear slices and drizzle with melted bittersweet chocolate, if you like.

PASSION FRUIT CUSTARDS

These delicate custards are accented by the seedless pulp of the passion fruit. Garnish each plate with a few seeds, along with some Red Berry Sauce (see page 60). This recipe makes 6.

2½ cups light cream	*4 egg yolks*
¼ cup granulated sugar	*⅓ cup seedless passion fruit pulp*
2 large eggs	

Heat the oven to 325°F.

Combine the cream and sugar in a saucepan over medium heat and simmer until the sugar dissolves. Beat the eggs and yolks together and stir in the warmed cream, then stir in the passion fruit. Pour the mixture into 6 ramekins.

Bake in a water bath in the middle of the oven about 35 minutes, until set and a knife inserted in the middle comes out clean. Let cool completely, then refrigerate at least 4 hours before serving.

CHILLED LIME SABAYON

For an attractive presentation, spoon the soft sabayon into hollowed lime cups and decorate the plate with a few red currants.

3 large eggs
½ cup fresh lime juice
1 tablespoon grated lime peel

½ cup granulated sugar
2 tablespoons unsalted butter, diced
½ cup heavy cream, whipped

Combine the egg yolks, lime juice, lime peel, and sugar in a medium bowl. Place the bowl over simmering water and whisk about 5 minutes, until the mixture is thick and creamy.

Remove the bowl from the heat and whisk in the butter pieces, a few at a time. Let the mixture cool, then chill. Fold in the whipped cream and refrigerate at least 4 hours before serving.

RHUBARB FOOL

Fools are a very versatile dessert. Serve this one alone, with macerated berries, or as a filling for Strawberry Shortcakes (see page 30).

2½ cups(12 ounces) rhubarb trimmed
and cut into ½inch slices
½ cup granulated sugar

1 teaspoon grated lemon peel
1¼ cups heavy cream, whipped

Combine the rhubarb, sugar, and lemon peel in a medium saucepan. Bring to a boil, then reduce the heat and simmer about 15 minutes, stirring often, until the rhubarb is very tender. Remove from the heat, let cool, and refrigerate until chilled.

Fold the rhubarb into the whipped cream. Return to the refrigerator and chill at least 4 hours before serving.

RASPBERRY CRÈME BRULÉES

Creamy custard, sweet raspberries, and crunchy caramel make this the ultimate dessert. Warning: this is not the most low-calorie dessert! This recipe makes 6.

1 cup (4 ounces) raspberries
5 egg yolks
¼ cup granulated sugar
1 teaspoon vanilla extract

2 cups heavy cream
½ cup packed brown sugar, strained
through a fine mesh sieve

Heat the oven to 300°F. Divide the raspberries equally between 6 ramekins.

Beat together the egg yolks, sugar, and vanilla. Bring the cream to a simmer. Gradually whisk the warm cream into the egg-yolk mixture. Pour this over the berries in the ramekins.

Bake the ramekins in a water bath in the middle of the oven for 40 minutes, until just barely set. Let cool; chill completely.

Just before serving, preheat the broiler to high. Sprinkle the tops of the custards evenly with brown sugar. Place the dishes under the broiler for a few minutes until the sugar melts; the sugar will harden as it cools.

COCONUT CRÈME CARAMEL

Smooth, creamy custard is infused with the exotic taste of coconut and accented with bittersweet caramel. This recipe makes 6.

2¼ cups half-and-half
¾ cup unsweetened flaked coconut, toasted
4 large eggs

½ cup granulated sugar
Pinch of salt
2 tablespoons coconut liqueur
½ teaspoon vanilla extract

FOR THE CARAMEL:
⅓ cup water
¾ cup granulated sugar

For the caramel, combine the water and sugar in a small saucepan. Slowly bring to a boil, stirring to dissolve the sugar. Once boiling, stop stirring and place a tight-fitting lid on top of the saucepan 1 to 2 minutes; this helps to dissolve any crystallized sugar on the sides of the pan. Cook until the sugar begins to caramelize. Swirl the saucepan over the heat until all is golden brown. Pour into 6 ramekins.

For the custard, heat the oven to 300°F. Combine the cream and coconut in a saucepan and bring to a boil; remove from the heat and cover for 30 minutes. Strain the mixture, pressing the coconut to extract all the cream. In a bowl, combine the remaining ingredients. Add the infused cream, stirring until combined. Pour into the ramekins. Bake in a water bath in the middle of the oven 35 to 45 minutes, until just set.

Below: Chilled Lime Sabayon

BLACKBERRY–WHITE CHOCOLATE PARFAITS

Any fresh berry will substitute for the blackberry. Serve the parfait in tall champagne flutes for a dramatic effect. This recipe makes 6.

2 cups (5 ounces) blackberries
2 tablespoons granulated sugar
1 teaspoon lemon juice
1 envelope unflavored gelatin
¼ cup water
4 large eggs, separated

½ cup confectioners' sugar, sifted
4 ounces white chocolate, chopped
6 tablespoons unsalted butter, at
room temperature
½ tablespoon vanilla extract
1 cup heavy cream, whipped

Toss the berries with the granulated sugar and lemon juice; set aside. Dissolve the gelatin in the water.

Beat the egg yolks and confectioners' sugar in a bowl set in a pan of simmering water for about 4 minutes, until very thick. Remove from the heat and stir in the white chocolate, butter, and dissolved gelatin, until the chocolate melts. Cool to room temperature.

In a separate bowl, beat the egg whites until stiff peaks form. Fold the beaten egg whites and whipped cream into the mousse mixture. Spoon or pipe into 6 glasses, layering with the fruit. Chill 4 to 6 hours before serving.

RASPBERRY–LEMON MOUSSE CAKE

Spring is here! No matter what the season this mousse cake is a real crowd pleaser. Serves 6.

½ baked Genoise Sponge (see page 58),
in one ½-inch layer
1 tablespoon orange-flavored liqueur
1 envelope unflavored gelatin
1 quantity Lemon Curd (see page 58),
made with ¼ cup extra sugar

3 egg whites
½ cup granulated sugar
⅔ cup heavy cream, whipped
to soft peaks
1 cup (4 ounces) raspberries

Fit the Genoise layer in a 9-inch springform pan. Sprinkle it with an orange-flavored liqueur, if desired; set aside.

Soften the gelatin in the water. Prepare the Lemon Curd according to directions. Add the gelatin to the curd and stir until dissolved. Cool until the curd is the consistency of unbeaten egg whites.

Beat the egg whites until soft peaks form. Continue beating, gradually adding the sugar, until stiff and glossy. Fold the egg whites and the whipped cream into the cooled lemon curd until blended. Gently fold in the raspberries. Pour the mixture into the pan. Refrigerate for about 6 hours, until firm, before removing the pan and serving.

LEMON MOUSSE QUENELLES VARIATION:
Prepare the lemon mousse without the raspberries and chill at least 4 hours, until set. To serve, dip 2 large spoons or an ice-cream scoop into warm water, then scoop up the mousse and mold into egg shapes. Serve with Red Berry Sauce (see page 60).

ORANGE SOUFFLÉ

Molly Stevens, the noted American food writer and instructor, adds a layer of fruit in the middle of the soufflé. It won't rise quite as much but it is well worth it. The pastry cream base of this soufflé can be made in advance; just bring it to room temperature before folding in the whites. Serves 6.

3 tablespoons all-purpose flour
½ cup granulated sugar
6 egg yolks
1 tablespoon grated orange peel
3 tablespoons orange-flavored liqueur

1 cup milk
8 egg whites
Pinch of salt
1 navel orange, sectioned, with all the
pith removed

Heat the oven to 375°F. Butter and sugar a 2-quart soufflé dish.

Combine the flour, half the sugar, the egg yolks, orange peel, and liqueur until well blended. In a saucepan, bring the milk to a simmer. Remove the pan from the heat and gradually add the yolk mixture, stirring constantly. Return the mixture to the heat and simmer, stirring constantly, until thick and bubbling. Transfer to a bowl and leave to cool to room temperature.

In a separate bowl, beat the egg whites with a pinch of salt until soft peaks form. Gradually add the remaining sugar and continue beating until stiff and glossy. Gently fold in the cooled pastry cream.

Spoon about one-third of the mixture into the prepared dish. Arrange orange sections on top. Spoon the remaining pastry cream over.

Bake in the middle of the oven about 35 minutes, until puffed and browned. Serve immediately.

MANGO FOOL

Is this a fool because any fool can make it, or because you would be a fool not to try this recipe?

2 large ripe mangoes, peeled and cut
into chunks
⅓ cup fresh orange juice
2 tablespoons fresh lime juice

Pinch of salt
½ to ¾ cup granulated sugar
1 cup heavy cream, whipped

TO DECORATE:
Sprig of mint
Toasted hazelnuts

Combine the mango chunks, orange and lime juices, salt, and ½ cup sugar in a food processor. Pulse until puréed. Taste and add more sugar if desired. Chill about 2 hours until very cold.

Fold the mango purée into the cream and chill at least 4 hours before serving. Garnish with a mint sprig and toasted hazelnuts.

ICE CREAMS, SORBETS, GRANITAS

The flavor of home-made ice cream is incomparable and it's much easier to make than you think. All you need are good-quality ingredients and an ice cream maker. Some of these recipes can even be made without a machine. All recipes serve 4 to 6.

APPLE CIDER GRANITA

The quality of the granita will depend on the cider you use. Freshly made cider is thick and rich in apple flavor. Using a large spoon and a scraping motion will yield the best icy results. This should serve 4 to 6.

6 cups freshly pressed apple cider
2 strips pared lemon peel, with all white pith removed
1 tablespoon apple brandy
2 cloves
1 cinnamon stick, 3 inches long

Place the cider in a saucepan over high heat and bring to a boil. Continue to boil until reduced to 4 cups.

Remove the pan from the heat. Stir in the lemon peel, cinnamon, and cloves. Cover and set aside until cooled to room temperature.

Remove the lemon peel and spices. Stir in the brandy. Pour the mixture into a shallow container and place in the freezer. Stir the granita every 30 minutes or so until the mixture begins to set. Freeze until completely set. To serve, scrape a spoon across the surface and transfer to chilled serving dishes.

LEMON SUCKER SORBET

Smooth and delicious, this sorbet truly lives up to its name. Of course, you can taste the syrup before freezing and adjust the sweetness. The addition of vodka prevents the mixture from freezing rock hard, but an egg white will achieve the same effect without adding alcohol.

1¼ cups granulated sugar
1¼ cups water
1½ cups fresh lemon juice
1 tablespoon vodka or 1 small egg white, lightly beaten

Combine the sugar, water, and lemon juice in a saucepan. Simmer, stirring, until the sugar dissolves. Remove the pan from the heat; set aside to cool completely.

Stir in the vodka or egg white, as preferred. Freeze the sorbet in an ice-cream maker according to the manufacturer's directions, or place it in a freezerproof bowl in the freezer, stirring frequently to disperse any ice crystals until set. To serve, let sit at room temperature for 5 minutes before spooning out.

WATERMELON ICE

Better than watermelon—no seeds! Check the fruit for sweetness and adjust the sugar as needed.

½ cup granulated sugar
½ cup water
3 sprigs of mint, or 1 sprig of rosemary (optional)
2 cups watermelon purée

Combine the sugar, water, and herb, if using, in a medium saucepan. Bring to a boil, stirring to dissolve the sugar. Remove from the heat; set aside to cool completely.

Remove the herb and stir in the watermelon purée. Pour the mixture into a shallow freezerproof container and place in the freezer. Stir every 30 minutes or so until the mixture begins to set. Freeze until completely set. To serve, scrape a spoon across the surface and transfer to chilled serving dishes.

PEACH ICE CREAM

Nothing could be more wonderful than peaches and cream—unless it's frozen!

4 ripe peaches, peeled, sliced, and mashed
1½ cups heavy cream
¾ cup granulated sugar
1 teaspoon vanilla extract

Combine the mashed peaches and their juices with the cream and sugar in the saucepan. Simmer, stirring to dissolve the sugar. Remove from the heat; set aside to cool completely. Stir in the vanilla.

Freeze in an ice-cream maker according to the manufacturer's directions, or place in a freezerproof container in the freezer, stirring frequently to disperse any ice crystals until set. To serve, let sit at room temperature for 5 minutes before spooning out.

PEACH MELBA VARIATION:
1 cup (4 ounces) raspberries
1 tablespoon granulated sugar
2 teaspoons Triple Sec

Combine the ingredients; leave to soak 30 minutes. Add the fruit and juices to the partially frozen ice cream. Return the ice cream to the freezer. Serve as above.

CRANBERRY SORBET

This sweet-tart dessert will quickly become a family favorite at holiday time. But keep cranberries in the freezer to enjoy this all year long!

¾ cup granulated sugar	1 tablespoon fresh lemon juice
½ cup water	Pinch of ground cinnamon
2½ cups (9 ounces) whole cranberries	1 tablespoon vodka, or 1 small egg white,
1½ cups cranberry juice	lightly beaten

Combine the sugar, water, and cranberries in a saucepan. Bring to a boil, stirring to dissolve the sugar, then boil for 3 minutes. Remove the pan from the heat; set aside to cool completely.

Process the cranberry mixture in a food processor, then strain it through a fine-mesh nylon sieve, discarding the pulp. Stir in the remaining ingredients.

Freeze the sorbet in an ice-cream maker according to the manufacturer's directions, or place in a freezerproof container in the freezer, stirring frequently to break up any ice crystals. Freeze until completely set. To serve, scrape a spoon across the surface and transfer to chilled serving dishes.

FRUITY ICE CREAM

Choose any one of the three fruit combinations to add to this rich and delicious vanilla ice cream.

VANILLA ICE CREAM

2½ cups half-and-half	¾ cup granulated sugar
6 egg yolks	1 teaspoon vanilla extract

NECTARINE-CINNAMON ICE CREAM:

1 cup finely chopped nectarine	1 teaspoon granulated sugar
¼ teaspoon ground cinnamon	½ teaspoon brandy

BANANA-RUM ICE CREAM:

1 large ripe banana, mashed	1 tablespoon dark rum
2 teaspoons light brown sugar	

STRAWBERRY ICE CREAM:

1 cup (about 8) mashed strawberries	½ teaspoon grated lemon peel
1 tablespoon granulated sugar	

To make the vanilla ice cream, heat the cream in a saucepan until just boiling. Beat together the egg yolks and sugar. Gradually beat in the heated cream, then pour the mixture back into the pan. Cook, stirring constantly, over medium heat until it has thickened and is 180°F on a candy thermometer. Strain the mixture and chill it thoroughly.

Meanwhile, combine all the ingredients for your chosen fruit addition; set aside for at least 1 hour.

When the ice-cream mixture is chilled, stir in the vanilla. Freeze in an ice-cream maker according to the manufacturer's directions, or place in a freezerproof container in the freezer, stirring frequently to disperse any ice crystals. Add the fruit and juices to the mixture half way through the freezing process. To serve, let sit at room temperature for 5 minutes before spooning out.

MANGO GRANITA

Cayenne pepper gives this granita a special zing. It's not too hot; just enough for a contrasting accent to the mellow mango flavor.

1 cup water	1½ tablespoons fresh lime juice
¾ cup granulated sugar	1 teaspoon grated lime peel
3 very ripe mangoes, peeled, seeded,	Pinch of cayenne pepper
puréed, and strained	Pinch of salt

Combine the water and the sugar in a saucepan. Bring to a boil, stirring to dissolve the sugar.

Remove the pan from the heat; set aside to cool completely. Stir in the remaining ingredients. Taste and add a little more cayenne, if desired.

Pour the mixture into a shallow container and place it in the freezer. Stir the granita every 30 minutes or so until the mixture begins to set. Return to the freezer until completely firm. To serve, scrape a spoon across the surface and transfer to chilled serving dishes.

PLUM–RASPBERRY SORBET

Choose very ripe plums and raspberries for a deep flavored sorbet.

¾ cup water	⅓ cup (1¼ ounces) raspberries
¾ cup granulated sugar	1½ tablespoons fresh lemon juice
1½ pounds plums, pitted and cut	1 tablespoon Triple Sec, or 1 small egg
into ¾-inch chunks	white, lightly beaten

Combine the water, sugar, plums, and raspberries in a saucepan. Cover and simmer, stirring often, until the fruit is very soft; this should take about 15 minutes. Pour the mixture through a fine-mesh nylon sieve; set liquid aside to cool completely. Stir in the remaining ingredients.

Freeze in an ice-cream maker according to the manufacturer's directions, or place in a freezerproof container in the freezer, stirring frequently to disperse any ice crystals. Freeze until completely set. To serve, scrape a spoon across the surface and transfer to chilled serving dishes.

Right: Cranberry Sorbet

CHOCOLATE–CHERRY ICE CREAM

The macerated cherries in this recipe are also delicious on their own, or triple the quantities and serve them with the Virginia Sponge (see page 24) instead of fresh berries. Here they are paired with rich chocolate ice cream.

FOR THE CHERRIES:

1 cup (8 ounces) pitted and chopped cherries *1 tablespoon brandy*
¼ cup granulated sugar

FOR THE ICE CREAM:

2½ cups light cream *½ teaspoon vanilla extract*
6 egg yolks *½ cup chopped toasted hazelnuts*
⅓ cup granulated sugar *(optional)*
8 ounces dark chocolate, finely chopped

Heat the cream to just below boiling point. In a medium bowl, whisk together the egg yolks and sugar.

Gradually whisk in the hot cream and chocolate, then pour the mixture back into the saucepan. Cook, stirring constantly, over medium heat until the mixture is thick and reaches 180°F on a candy thermometer. Strain the mixture into a bowl and refrigerate it until completely chilled.

Combine the cherry ingredients; leave to stand while the cream cools.

When the mixture is chilled, stir in the vanilla. Freeze the cooled ice-cream mixture in an ice-cream maker according to the manufacturer's directions or place in a freezerproof container in the freezer, stirring frequently to disperse any ice crystals.

Half way through the freezing process, add the chopped cherries and their juices, and hazelnuts if using, to the chocolate mixture and freeze until set. To serve, let sit at room temperature for 5 minutes before spooning out.

PIÑA COLADA ICE CREAM

Just top with toasted coconut and you are half way to the Caribbean! Allowing the yogurt to drain gives the finished product a smoother consistency—not essential but preferred.

1½ cups plain low-fat yogurt *⅔ cup finely chopped, well-drained*
1⅔ cups half-and-half or milk *pineapple*
⅔ cup granulated sugar *1 tablespoon dark rum*

Place the yogurt in a cheesecloth-lined sieve set over a bowl for about 1 hour to drain off some of the liquid.

In a saucepan, combine the milk and sugar and simmer, stirring to dissolve the sugar. Transfer to a bowl; set aside to cool. Stir in the strained yogurt, the pineapple, and the rum.

Freeze in an ice-cream maker according to the manufacturer's directions, or place in a freezerproof container in the freezer, stirring frequently to disperse any ice crystals. Freeze until set. To serve, let sit at room temperature for 5 minutes before spooning out.

PINK GRAPEFRUIT SORBET

Refreshing and light, yet loaded with grapefruit flavor—perfect for a winter dinner intermezzo or a summertime cooler.

4 large pink or ruby red grapefruits *1 tablespoon fresh lemon juice*
1⅓ cups granulated sugar *Pinch of salt*
1 tablespoon vodka, or 1 small egg white,
lightly beaten

Cut 3 large strips of peel from the grapefruits, removing all the white pith. Squeeze the grapefruits and combine the juice with the sugar and peel in a saucepan. Bring to a boil, stirring to dissolve the sugar. Remove the pan from the heat; set aside at least 30 minutes for the juice to infuse and cool completely. Remove the peel and stir in the vodka or egg white, lemon juice, and salt.

Freeze in an ice-cream maker according to the manufacturer's directions, or place in a freezerproof container in the freezer, stirring frequently to disperse any ice crystals. Freeze until completely set. To serve, scrape a spoon across the surface and transfer to chilled serving dishes.

MINT–ORANGE TEA SORBET

Tea sorbet is as light and refreshing as the iced drink. The addition of mint and orange makes it truly special.

1 cup granulated sugar *1½ cups fresh orange juice*
2½ cups water *1 tablespoon orange-flavored liqueur*
6 tea bags *1 tablespoon vodka*
4 sprigs of mint

Combine the sugar and water in a saucepan and bring to a boil, then simmer, stirring, until the sugar dissolves. Remove the pan from the heat. Add the tea bags and mint sprigs and let cool for 30 minutes.

Remove the tea bags and mint sprigs before stirring in the orange juice, liqueur, and vodka.

Freeze the sorbet in an ice-cream maker according to the manufacturer's directions, or place in a freezerproof container in the freezer, stirring frequently to break up any ice crystals. Freeze until completely set. To serve, scrape a spoon across the surface and transfer to chilled serving dishes.

LIME ICE CREAM

Honey sweetens and mellows the lime flavor in this creamy treat.

2 tablespoons honey *2 teaspoons grated lime peel*
¼ cup granulated sugar *2 cups light cream*
½ cup fresh lime juice

Combine the honey, sugar, and lime juice and peel in a saucepan. Simmer, stirring to dissolve the sugar, then remove the pan from the heat and leave the mixture to cool completely. Stir in the cream. Freeze and serve as for Piña Colada Ice Cream (left).

Right Chocolate–Cherry Ice Cream

FRESH FRUIT AND COMPOTES

Here is a selection of light and easy fruit desserts. The recipes are easy to follow and the results are stunning, making them the perfect choice for a sophisticated finish to an elegant meal.

POACHED SECKLE PEARS

Seckels are the smallest of pears. Dainty and delicious, they can also be costly. Feel free to substitute larger Comice or Anjou, cutting them in half. The poaching time will vary depending on the size and ripeness of the pears. Serves 2.

5 cups fresh apple cider
½ cup packed light brown sugar
2 cinnamon sticks, about 3 inches long
½ vanilla bean, split
6 firm Seckel pears or 3 Comice, peeled and cored from the bottom

Combine all the ingredients except for the pears in a medium saucepan just big enough to hold the pears when they are required. Simmer, stirring, until the sugar dissolves.

Add the pears and cover with a piece of parchment paper to help the fruit cook more evenly and prevent discoloring. Simmer 10 to 25 minutes, turning the pears over occasionally, until they are tender. Remove the pan from the heat and leave the pears to cool to room temperature. Cover the pan and refrigerate until the pears are throughly chilled.

Before serving, transfer the pears to a serving dish. Place the pan over high heat and boil the poaching liquid until thick and syrupy.

Serve the pears drizzled with some of the liquid.

APRICOT VARIATION: Stuff each pear cavity with 1 or 2 dried apricots before poaching. Continue as directed above.

STEWED STONE FRUIT

Make use of early, firmer fruit for this light dessert. Garnish the fruit with a chiffonade of fresh mint leaves just before serving. Serves 4.

2 ripe-yet-firm peaches
3 ripe-yet-firm plums
4 ripe-yet-firm apricots
2 ripe-yet-firm nectarines
2 tablespoons fresh lemon juice
1¾ cup granulated sugar
1 cup water
3 sprigs of fresh mint

Cut all the fruit into ¾-inch-thick sections—there's no need to peel. Toss with the lemon juice; set aside.

Combine the sugar and water in a large saucepan. Bring to a simmer, stirring to dissolve the sugar. Add the fruit and simmer for about 10 minutes, stirring occasionally, until all the fruit is just tender. Remove from the heat and stir in the mint sprigs.

Leave to cool to room temperature; cover and chill overnight before serving.

WINTER FRUIT COMPOTE

Spoon this wintry treat over a piece of Orange Sunshine Cake (see page 18) or serve with a dollop of whipped cream. Serves 6 to 8.

2 cups dry white wine
½ vanilla bean, split
8 ounces dried Black Mission figs, cut in half
8 ounces dried Calamyrna figs, cut in half
1½ cups dried apricots, cut in half
1 cup golden raisins
1 cup fresh whole cranberries
¾ to 1 cup granulated sugar
1 cup chopped dates

Combine the wine and vanilla bean in a large saucepan. Add the figs, apricots, and golden raisins. Simmer about 7 minutes. Add the cranberries and simmer 10 minutes longer, until the fruit is tender. Stir in ¾ cup sugar, stirring until the sugar dissolves. Taste and add more sugar if neccesary. Remove from the heat. Stir in the dates; leave to cool to room temperature.

Cover the compote and refrigerate for at least 1 day to let flavors mellow.

ALL–BERRY RUMPOT

The concept of a rumpot is to combine equal amounts of the freshest fruit and sugar, cover the fruit with alcohol and leave it to steep in a dark spot. As the summer progresses, keep adding to the rumpot; layering more fresh berries, sugar, and rum. Make sure the berries show no signs of mold or the whole pot will be in jeopardy! Serve with cream or vanilla ice cream. Serves 10.

About 12 ounces each: strawberries,
raspberries, blackberries, blueberries,
and red currants

About 4 pounds granulated sugar
About 2 bottles good-quality rum,
brandy, or vodka

Choose a large glass or ceramic jar with a tight-fitting lid. Wash and dry it thoroughly.

Select only the freshest, sweetest berries available. Remember, you want to add different berries to the rumpot as the summer progresses. Carefully rinse and dry one type of berry at a time, removing stems and seeds as necessary. Weigh the fruit and add it to the container. Sprinkle over an equal amount of granulated sugar and cover with the rum, brandy, or vodka. If the fruit floats to the top, cover with a piece of crumpled parchment paper (if the fruit is exposed to the air it will spoil).

Fit the lid on tightly and place container in a dark spot. Steep for at least 3 weeks, but continue to add more fruit, sugar, and rum as fresh berries come into season. The rumpot should last for months if properly managed.

APPLESAUCE

This applesauce is on the chunky side but it can be passed through a fine-mesh nylon sieve or a food mill for a smoother sauce. Use the basic sauce for other recipes, but be sure to try the spiced version. This recipe makes about 3 cups.

2½ pounds firm, flavorsome apples
½ cup water
1 tablespoon lemon juice

Combine the ingredients in a heavy saucepan. Simmer for about 40 minutes, stirring frequently, until the apples are very soft. Leave to cool slightly before mashing or sieving if required. The applesauce can be served warm or chilled.

VARIATION:
¼ cup packed light brown sugar
½ teaspoon ground cinnamon

1 teaspoon vanilla extract
3 tablespoons unsalted butter

After cooking the basic sauce, stir in these spicy ingredients.

MELON COMPOTE

Perfectly ripe fruit is the key to this light and refreshing dessert. Make sure to choose at least two different colors of melon—ambrosia and honeydew are nice. Serves 6 to 8.

3 ripe melons
⅓ cup fresh lime juice

3 tablespoons granulated sugar
2 tablespoons thinly sliced fresh mint leaves

TO DECORATE:
Sprig of fresh mint

Remove and discard the inner seeds from the melons.

Using a large melon baller, cut balls from each of the melons. Toss these with the remaining ingredients.

Refrigerate the compote for at least 4 hours before serving, decorated with fresh mint.

Right: *All–Berry Rumpot*

Above: Papaya–Pineapple Compote

PAPAYA–PINEAPPLE COMPOTE

A truly tropical delight! Feel free to decorate the fruit slices with passion fruit pulp, with or without the seeds. Serves 4.

2 papayas, peeled, seeded, and sliced
1 ripe pineapple, peeled, cored,
and sliced

3 kiwi fruits, peeled and sliced

FOR THE SYRUP:
2½ cups fresh orange juice
½ cup granulated sugar
2 stalks lemongrass, trimmed and
each cut into 3 pieces

One 2-inch piece of gingeroot, peeled and
thinly sliced

Combine the syrup ingredients in a saucepan and simmer, stirring constantly, until the sugar dissolves. Bring to a boil and reduce the liquid by half—the syrup should thicken. Remove from the heat; set aside to cool completely. Cover and chill until required.

Arrange the fruit on plates and drizzle with the cooled syrup. Garnish with passion fruit pulp and mint sprigs.

CITRUS TERRINE

The quality of this dessert depends solely on the quality of the fruit. Now is not the time to skimp—buy the best and console yourself in the fact that it's fat-free! Serves 6.

3 grapefruits—a combination of pink
and yellow is most attractive
5 navel oranges
4 blood oranges

6 to 8 strawberries, rinsed and hulled
1 tablespoon + 1 teaspoon unflavored
gelatin
1 tablespoon chopped fresh mint

Rinse a 6-cup loaf pan with cold water; set aside.

With a sharp knife, cut away all the peel and pith from the citrus fruits. Holding the fruits one at a time over a medium bowl to catch the juice and fruit, cut out sections; discard the membrane skeletons.

Drain off all the juice from the sections, reserving 1 cup. Spread the sections onto a triple thickness of paper towels. Warm the reserved juice and dissolve the gelatin in this. Cool to room temperature.

Sprinkle the mint over the fruit sections. Arrange half of the sections in the pan. Line the strawberries along the middle, making sure the fruit is tightly packed. Add the remaining sections of citrus fruit. Pour in the cooled juice mixture. Tap the pan gently on the counter to release any air bubbles.

Cover the pan with plastic wrap and refrigerate at least 6 hours, until set.

To serve, rub a warmed towel around the pan and loosen the sides of the terrine with a sharp, thin knife. Quickly invert the terrine onto a serving plate, shake gently (repeat if necessary) and lift off the pan. Cut into 1-inch-thick slices. Serve immediately.

BAKED APPLES

Delicious any time of the year! Adults and children alike love these, and they're great as an after-school snack, too. Use Rome, Cortland, or Golden Delicious apples. Serves 4.

4 large baking apples
⅓ cup chopped dried fruit
2 tablespoons packed light brown sugar
2 tablespoons shredded coconut, toasted

½ cup water
¼ cup honey
¼ teaspoon ground cinnamon

Heat the oven to 400°F. Core the apples, leaving the bottoms intact. Peel off the top third of the skin. Mix together the fruit, sugar, and coconut, and fill the apples with this mixture. Arrange the apples standing upright in a 9-inch baking dish.

Mix together the water, honey, and cinnamon, and spoon over the apples. Bake the apples in the middle of the oven, basting occasionally, 45 to 60 minutes, depending on their size, until they are tender but not mushy. Serve hot or warm.

BRANDIED PEACHES IN PHYLLO CUPS

These versatile cups can easily hold any macerated fruit. Consider filling them with Rhubarb Fool (see page 41) and decorating them with kiwi fruit slices. Or, serve them with a dollop of whipped cream. This recipe makes 6.

1 cup sliced almonds, toasted	*⅓ cup granulated sugar*
6 tablespoons unsalted butter	*1 tablespoon fresh lemon juice*
¼ cup honey	*½ cup brandy*
6 sheets phyllo dough, thawed if frozen	*½ teaspoon ground cinnamon*
1½ pounds peaches, peeled and sliced	

Heat the oven to 325°F. Lightly grease 6 ramekins. Finely chop about two-thirds of the almonds.

In a small saucepan, combine the butter and honey. Simmer, stirring, until the butter is melted and the mixture blended.

Work with one sheet of phyllo dough at a time, keeping the remaining dough covered with plastic wrap or a damp towel. Brush each sheet of dough with the butter mixture and sprinkle with about 2 tablespoons chopped nuts. Place the next layer of dough on top and repeat the process with the remaining nuts, butter mixture, and dough. Cut the stack into six 5½-inch squares.

Press the dough squares into the ramekins, gently crinkling the edges to form a cup shape. Bake in the middle of the oven about 20 minutes, until golden brown. Remove from the oven and leave to cool completely before lifting out of the ramekins.

Meanwhile, combine the peaches, sugar, lemon juice, brandy, and cinnamon in a saucepan over medium heat. Simmer gently, stirring, until the sugar dissolves and the peaches are warm. Remove from the heat; set aside. (The peaches can be served warm or at room temperature.)

Place one phyllo cup on each serving dish and arrange the brandied peaches in them. Decorate with the remaining toasted almonds.

CHOCOLATE–STUFFED PEARS

Chocolate ganache filling with poached pears is simply to die for. Any leftover ganache can be heated and drizzled over the pears.
Serves 4.

⅓ cup heavy cream	*4 whole pears, poached and drained*
4 ounces bittersweet chocolate, chopped	*(see Poached Pears, page 56)*

Heat the cream to simmering point. Pour it over the chocolate and stir together until melted. Leave to cool, then chill until firm. This is the ganache.

Using an apple corer, core each pear from the bottom. Dry the hollow of each pear with paper towels. Spoon the ganache into a pastry bag fitted with a wide, plain tip. Pipe the ganache into the hollows until they are filled. Cover and chill the pears until it is time to serve.

POACHED APPLES WITH APRICOTS

Firm, tart apples are the ones to use here. Granny Smith is a good choice as it is almost always available. Pears are easily substituted. Serves 6.

5 cups apricot nectar	*½ vanilla bean, split*
4 ounces dried apricots	*2 strips lemon peel, white pith removed*
¾ cup apricot jam	*1 to 2 tablespoons granulated sugar (optional)*
1 cinnamon stick, 3 inches long	*6 small, firm apples, peeled and cored*
Mascarpone cheese, to serve	

Combine all the ingredients except the sugar and apples in a saucepan just big enough to hold the apples in a single layer when they are required. Bring the mixture to a simmer. Taste for sweetness and add 1 to 2 tablespoons sugar if needed.

Add the apples to the simmering liquid. Place a circle of parchment or waxed paper directly onto the surface to help the fruit cook more evenly and prevent discoloring. Simmer the apples 15 to 20 minutes, turning them over occasionally, until just tender; set aside to cool completely.

Before serving, remove the apples from the poaching liquid and return the saucepan to the heat. Bring the poaching liquid to a boil and reduce until the flavor is concentrated. Place each apple in a bowl and serve with the syrup, warm or cold, and a dollop of mascarpone cheese.

Below: *Brandied Peaches in Phyllo Cups*

POACHED PEACHES IN ZINFANDEL

This is the perfect recipe for those first peaches of the season, which sometimes lack flavor. It also makes for an elegant presentation; just drizzle with syrup and garnish with a mint sprig. Serves 6.

4 cups red zinfandel wine
¾ to 1 cup granulated sugar
1 cinnamon stick, 3 inches long

4 sprigs fresh mint
3 strips lemon peel, white pith removed
6 peaches, firm but not hard

Combine all the ingredients except the peaches in a saucepan just big enough to hold the peaches in a single layer when they are required. Bring to a simmer, stirring to dissolve the sugar. Taste and add the sugar, if necessary.

Add the peaches and cover with a circle of parchment paper to help the fruit cook more evenly and prevent discoloring. Simmer 15 to 20 minutes, until the peaches are tender. Remove the pan from the heat; set aside for the peaches and poaching liquid to cool completely.

Before serving, remove the peaches from the poaching liquid. Bring the liquid to a boil and reduce until the flavor is concentrated. Serve at once and drizzle the hot liquid over the peaches, or set aside to cool and serve later.

PEAR DUMPLINGS

Easier than pie—pastry is wrapped around ripe pears stuffed with toasted nuts. Child's play—but adult's delight! Serves 4.

½ cup toasted and chopped walnuts
3 tablespoons packed light brown sugar
¾ teaspoon ground cinnamon
4 firm, ripe pears, peeled and cored from the bottom

2 egg yolks
1 tablespoon heavy cream
1 quantity Classic Pie and Tart Crust (see page 61), unbaked

Heat the oven to 375°F. Line a baking sheet with parchment paper.

Toss together the nuts, sugar, and cinnamon. Fill each pear with the mixture. Whisk together the egg yolks and cream; set aside.

Roll half of the dough at a time on a lightly floured surface to a ⅛-inch thickness. Cut out four 6- to 8-inch squares, depending on the size of the pears. Place one pear at a time in the middle of a dough square. Bring the dough corners up to the top, brush them with the egg and cream mixture, and press the seams to seal. The pears will look like four-cornered hats. Transfer the pear to the prepared baking sheet. Repeat this process with the remaining dough and pears.

Brush the dough with the remaining glaze and decorate the outside with leaves or stems cut out from any remaining dough. Brush again with the glaze.

Bake the pears in the middle of the oven about 40 minutes, until the pastry is golden brown and the pears are tender if you test them with a skewer.

POACHED PEARS

Classic and traditional, this recipe is the basis for many desserts. The pears are also delicious served with Red Berry Sauce (see page 60). Serves 4.

2½ cups water
1 cup granulated sugar
2 strips lemon peel, all white pith removed
2 strips orange peel, all white pith removed

1 vanilla bean, split
4 firm, ripe pears, peeled, cored, and cut in half lengthwise

Combine all the ingredients except the pears in a saucepan just big enough to hold the pears in a single layer when they are required. Simmer, stirring, until the sugar dissolves. Add the pear halves and cover with a piece of parchment paper to help the fruit cook more evenly and prevent discoloring. Simmer 12 to 15 minutes, until the pears are just tender.

Remove the pan from the heat. Leave the pears to cool completely in the poaching liquid. Cover and refrigerate until ready to serve.

STEWED RHUBARB WITH GRAPEFRUIT AND STRAWBERRIES

Rich and saucy, this dessert is surprising low in fat. Serves 4.

¾ cup granulated sugar
1 pound rhubarb, trimmed and cut into 1-inch chunks
1 sprig of rosemary
3 strips lemon peel

1 cup water
1 pint (12 ounces) strawberries, rinsed, hulled, and quartered
1 large grapefruit, peeled and sectioned

Combine the sugar, rhubarb, rosemary, lemon peel and water in a large saucepan. Simmer for about 5 minutes, stirring frequently, until the rhubarb is just tender. Remove the pan from the heat and add the strawberries.

Leave to cool to room temperature before gently stirring in the grapefruit sections. Cover and chill overnight.

Serve chilled or at room temperature.

Right: Poached Peaches in Zinfandel

BASICS

These are used throughout the book and are cross-referenced in their appropriate recipes. Be sure to read through the pastry tips on page 61 before you begin any pie or tart recipes.

GENOISE SPONGE

This makes one 9-inch cake.

¾ cup all-purpose flour
Pinch of salt
4 large eggs
⅔ cup granulated sugar

¾ teaspoon vanilla extract
3 tablespoons unsalted butter, melted and
cooled

Preheat the oven to 350°F. Grease and flour a 9-inch cake pan.

Sift the flour and the salt together. In a separate bowl, beat the eggs until foamy. Slowly add the sugar and continue beating until very thick and pale. Stir in the vanilla extract.

Using a large metal spoon, fold in the sifted flour, then gently fold in the butter. Pour the batter into the prepared pan and smooth the surface. Bake in the middle of the oven 35 to 40 minutes, until golden and the top springs back when touched.

Leave to cool 5 minutes in the pan, then remove from the pan and invert onto a rack to cool completely.

GRAPEFRUIT CURD

A tasty alternative to the more-traditional lemon curd, this makes a fabulous accompaniment to fresh berries, as well as the "Grape-Fruit" Curd Tart (see page 20). This makes about 1½ cups.

¾ cup grapefruit juice
4 egg yolks
½ cup granulated sugar

1 tablespoon grated grapefruit peel
3 tablespoons unsalted butter

Follow the instructions for making a Lemon Curd (see above right). Keep chilled and use within 3 days.

LEMON CURD

Use this tart and tasty curd as the filling for a summer tart, the basis of lemon mousse or in Raspberry–Lemon Mousse Cake (see page 42). This makes about 1½ cups.

5 large egg yolks
⅔ cup granulated sugar
½ cup fresh lemon juice

1 teaspoon grated lemon peel
Pinch of salt
4 tablespoons (½ stick) unsalted butter

Combine all the ingredients except the butter in the top of a double boiler and place it over simmering water. (If you don't have a double boiler, use a heatproof bowl placed over a saucepan of simmering water.) Stir the mixture often until it thickens, which should take about 15 minutes, or slightly longer if you aren't using a double boiler.

Remove the pan from the heat and stir in the butter. Transfer to another bowl. Cover the surface with plastic wrap and refrigerate until cold. Keep chilled and use within 3 days.

PASTRY CREAM

This should make about 1¾ cups.

1½ cups milk
4 egg yolks
⅓ cup granulated sugar
2 tablespoons cornstarch

1 teaspoon vanilla extract
2 tablespoons unsalted butter
at room temperature

Bring the milk to a boil in a saucepan over medium-high heat. Meanwhile, in a bowl, whisk together the egg yolks, sugar, and cornstarch until well blended. Gradually whisk in the hot milk. Pour the mixture back into the pan.

Return the saucepan to medium-low heat and simmer, stirring constantly, until the mixture is boiling and thickened.

Remove the pan from the heat and strain the mixture into a medium bowl. Stir in the vanilla and butter. Cover the surface with plastic wrap and refrigerate until well chilled. Keep chilled and use within 3 days.

Above: *Peach Ice Cream (see page 44)*

PRETZEL CRUST

Makes enough for one 9-inch pie plate.

1 cup finely crushed salted pretzels
⅓ cup granulated sugar
½ cup (1 stick) unsalted butter, melted

Toss all the ingredients together. Press them into the bottom of a 9-inch pie plate and slightly up the sides to make a rim around the edge. Freeze until firm; use frozen.

RED BERRY SAUCE

This makes about 1¼ cups.

12 ounces raspberries, strawberries,   *2 tablespoons Chambord or similar liqueur*
or a combination, fresh or frozen   *1 to 3 tablespoons fresh lemon juice*
⅓ to ½ cup granulated sugar

Combine the berries, ⅓ cup of the sugar, the liqueur, and 1 tablespoon lemon juice in a food processor and purée until smooth. Pass the sauce through a fine mesh nylon strainer, pressing to extract all the pulp from the seeds. Taste, and adjust the sugar or lemon juice if necessary.

SHORTCAKES

Makes 8 shortcakes.

3 cups all-purpose flour   *½ cup shortening, chilled and cut*
¼ cup granulated sugar   *into pieces*
1 teaspoon salt   *1 cup buttermilk*
1 tablespoon + 2 teaspoons baking powder   *1 teaspoon vanilla extract*

Heat the oven to 400°F. Lightly butter a baking sheet or line it with parchment paper.

Combine the flour, sugar, salt, and baking powder in a medium bowl. Cut in the shortening until coarse crumbs form.

Pour in the buttermilk and vanilla. Gently toss until the mixture forms a dough. On a lightly floured surface, pat the dough into a rectangle ¾ inch thick. Cut into 8 squares and transfer to the prepared baking sheet.

Bake the shortcakes in the middle of the oven 15 to 20 minutes, until golden.

SWEET TART PASTRY

Makes enough for one 9-inch tart shell.

1¼ cups all-purpose flour   *1 egg yolk*
¼ cup granulated sugar   *½ teaspoon vanilla extract*
Pinch of salt
½ cup (1 stick) unsalted butter, chilled and
cut into pieces

Place the flour, sugar, and salt in a food processor and pulse to combine. Add the butter and pulse until the mixture forms coarse crumbs. Add the egg yolk and vanilla and pulse again just until a dough forms. Gather the dough into a ball and flatten. Wrap it in plastic wrap and chill for about 1 hour.

Roll out the dough on a lightly floured surface or between 2 sheets of waxed paper. Line the bottom and sides of a 9-inch pie plate or tart pan with a removable bottom. Use your finger to press the dough into place. Crimp or flatten the edge. Trim off any excess.

To bake blind, freeze the dough in the pan for 45 minutes. Meanwhile, heat the oven to 400°F. Bake in the middle of the oven 15 to 20 minutes, until golden brown.

CLASSIC PIE AND TART CRUST

Makes enough for two 9-inch pie or tart shells, or one 9-inch double-crust pie. Freeze the unbaked shell for up to 3 months; use frozen. The baked shell can kept for one day, tightly wrapped.

2½ cups all-purpose flour
½ teaspoon salt
½ cup shortening, chilled and cut into pieces
4 tablespoons butter, chilled and diced
2 teaspoons lemon juice
3 to 5 tablespoons very cold water

Combine the flour and salt in a food processor. Add the shortening and butter and pulse until coarse crumbs form. Add the lemon juice and 3 tablespoons water. Pulse these until the dough forms; it may be necessary to add an additional 1 to 2 tablespoons of water, but use these sparingly. Shape the dough into 2 flat discs, wrap them in plastic wrap and refrigerate for at least 1 hour before use.

FOR A SINGLE-CRUST PIE OR TART SHELL:
Roll out one of the dough discs between 2 pieces of waxed paper or on a lightly floured surface to about ⅛ inch thick. Lift the dough into the pie plate or a tart pan with a removable bottom. Use your fingers to gently mold the dough into the dish. Crimp or flatten the dough and trim off any excess.

Freeze the pastry for at least 30 minutes. Meanwhile, heat the oven to 400°F. Remove the dough from the freezer and line it with a large piece of foil and fill it with pie weights or dried beans. Bake on the middle shelf 15 minutes. Remove the foil and weights or beans and continue baking 5 to 10 minutes longer, until golden brown. This technique is called blind baking.

FOR A TWO-CRUST PIE:
Do not bake the dough blind. Roll the second half of the dough a bit thicker than the bottom. Fill the pie or tart and cover it with the second piece of dough. Crimp the edges together and trim off any excess. Cut vent holes in the top crust. Bake following the recipe.

FOR A LATTICE TOP:
Roll out and line a pie pan with half the dough, but do not crimp. Roll out the remaining dough into a 12 x 8-inch rectangle. Cut into eight 1-inch strips; cut 2 of the strips in half. On a floured parchment-lined baking sheet, arrange half the pastry strips about 1½ inches apart; use the short strips for the sides. Turn the paper 90° and, beginning in the middle, weave long strips into bottom strips; again, use the short ones for the sides. Chill the dough until firm. Fill the pie and gently invert the lattice on top of the filling. Trim and crimp the edges.

GALETTE DOUGH

For Spicy Galette Dough, add ½ teaspoon ground cinnamon and a pinch of ground nutmeg to the dry ingredients.

2 cups all-purpose flour
2 tablespoons granulated sugar
¼ teaspoon salt
10 tablespoons cold unsalted butter, cut into pieces
½ cup very cold water

Combine flour, sugar, and salt in a bowl. Rub in the butter with your fingers or cut it in with a pastry blender until coarse crumbs form. Add the water and toss it gently until the pastry holds together. Shape it into a flattened disc and refrigerate for at least 1 hour before using.

PASTRY WORK MADE EASY

Working with pastry dough can flummox even the most skilled professional. But don't give up, help is here! By following a few basic rules along with a few tricks of the trade, even the most difficult dough will yield high-quality results. Concentrate on the four basic elements of pastry making: the mixing, the rolling, the transferring, and the baking.

Work the ingredients together quickly, using your fingertips—no hot, sweaty palms, please. Without overworking the dough, gently shape it into a flat, round disc (if making a double crust, first divide the dough), wrap in plastic wrap, and refrigerate at least 1 hour or up to two days. This rest period relaxes the gluten and makes rolling a breeze.

When ready to roll, choose a cool surface (marble or stainless steel are the best), away from the heat of the stovetop or oven. Lightly flour the surface—too much flour will toughen the dough. If the dough is particularly fragile or time is of the essence, roll out the pastry between two pieces of waxed paper. This method allows for less flour and quick turns, all of which speeds the process along. Hold the rolling pin over the middle of the dough and, gently but firmly, push down away from the middle. Continue turning the dough clockwise and rolling, while lightly dusting with flour as needed until it is the desired thickness. Keep in mind that an even thickness is the goal for the best results.

Transfering the dough to a pie plate or pan can be tricky. Always make sure the container is ready to go. If using the paper method, slide a baking sheet underneath the rolled-out dough and place on top of the container. Gently tug the bottom piece of paper and the baking sheet away, leaving the dough on top. Or, lightly flour the top of the dough and, using no pressure, roll it around the pin, then gently unroll on top of the pie or tart container. Press the dough into the container, using just your fingertips. Don't stretch the dough, as it will shrink during baking. In a tart pan, level the top by rolling the rolling pin over the top edge, or trim with a knife if using a pie plate.

At this point, the dough case can be frozen, or it can filled and baked, or baked blind (see Classic Crust recipe). In most cases, the dough should not be pricked at the bottom, especially if the filling is runny. Whether the recipe calls for a fully baked, partially baked, or unbaked crust, pop it in the freezer 15 to 20 minutes before baking. This is a foolproof method to avoid pastry shrinkage during baking.

RECIPE INDEX

ACKNOWLEDGMENTS

I would like to thank my husband, Chris, and my children, Alex and Tierney, for their patience and love during the busy time of preparing this book. They shared my excitement and enthusiasm for the project and kept the family going while I was cooking!

I would like to thank my terrific support team: the glue that held this writer's life together. Julie Fulop ran the house with confidence and love. Emily Head wrestled with the computer and won! Ann Mileti, Wendy Hyman, and Jennifer Smith tested many, many recipes and offered their thoughtful insights to improve them. Many thanks to the staff at *Fine Cooking Magazine*, who graciously tolerated a slightly distracted recipe tester. Kudos to my chief taste testers: Tim Johnson; Chris, Alex, and Tierney Dodge; Ed and Ann Mileti; Andrew and Harriet Powell; and Mrs. W. S. Mays—their refined palates and opinions were much appreciated.

Many thanks my friend and food idol Martha Holmberg for bringing the project to me, and to Charlotte Umanoff, whose arrival gave me the time necessary to complete the task.

I would like to thank Grace Bell, Barbara Powell, and Ann Mileti for contributing their delicious recipes. And, of course, my produce gurus, Nate and Hector at Hay Day in Westport, Connecticut, for sharing their fruit wisdom and tolerating my endless questions and requests!

Last but not least, my deepest thanks to Laura Washburn, my editor at Weidenfeld & Nicolson, who led me through the maze of my first book, Robin Matthews for his sumptuous photographs, Roisin Nield for evoking a beautiful atmosphere, and Emma Patmore, for creating the glorious food that brings the book to life!

First published in the United States of America in 1997 by
RIZZOLI INTERNATIONAL PUBLICATIONS, INC.
300 Park Avenue South, New York,
NY 10010

First published in Great Britain in 1997 by George Weidenfeld & Nicolson Limited
The Orion Publishing Group

Text copyright © 1997 Weidenfeld & Nicolson
Photographs copyright © 1997 Robin Matthews

ISBN 0-8478-2018-1
LC 96-71422

Stylist: Roisin Nield
Home Economist: Emma Patmore
Designed by Paul Cooper

Printed and bound in Italy